W9-BVU-521

RESCUES
The Lives of Heroes

RESCUES

The Lives of Heroes

MICHAEL LESY

Farrar   Straus   Giroux

NEW YORK

Library of Congress Cataloging-in-Publication Data
Lesy, Michael.
Rescues : the lives of heroes / Michael Lesy.
p.   cm.
Includes index.
1. United States—Biography.   2. Biography—20th century.
3. Heroes—United States—Biography.   I. Title.
CT220.L47   1991   973'.099—dc20   [B]   90-43000

For the ones who died

Acknowledgments

WITHDRAWN

THANKS TO LIZ for listening to me read; to Liza Nelson, Alice Alexander, and Greil Marcus for reading what I wrote and telling me what they thought; to Cormac McCarthy, Aristide Caratzas, Jeremy Zwelling, John McDermott, Nick Lemann, Susan Rosenberg, and Robert Lifton for their advice.

To the Marguerite Eyer Wilbur Foundation for its financial support.

To the staffs and officers of the Carnegie Hero Fund, the MacArthur Foundation, and the Congressional Medal of Honor Society for helping me contact their members or recipients.

To General Raymond G. Davis and Colonel William E. Barber, both United States Marine Corps, retired, for what they told me about themselves and the war in Korea; to Temple Grandon, Charles Hart, Deanna Luscre, and Marge Truax, all members of the Autism Society of America, for what they taught me about autism; to the Reverend Ed King, Lilli Baxter, and Geri Allen for educating me about the struggle for civil rights; to Frances and Chester Sliwa and to John Corcoran of *Fighter Magazine* for helping me to understand and

Acknowledgments

write about the Alliance of Guardian Angels and its founder.

To Tom Baxter at the *Atlanta Journal and Constitution* and Drayton Scott, Jr., at Merrill Lynch for their professional assistance; to Lee Kravitz and Tammy Hanneman for their hospitality; to Lee Ann Lloyd for deciphering my handwriting.

I'm grateful to you all.

Author's Note: In "Common Men," Timothy Chorcoran's last name was changed, at his request, to protect his privacy.

Contents

RESCUES

The Lives of Heroes

Prologue

THERE WERE three hundred of us, all boys. I was thirteen. Eisenhower was in the White House and we were in chapel. It was an enormous Palladian room, lit by a wall of arched windows, the ceiling forty feet above us, the pews, where we sat, painted the color of sweet cream trimmed with black walnut, thirty rows of boys dressed in jackets and ties, ranked by age on either side of an aisle. Behind us, high above us, was the organ loft; to our right, a huge blank wall, plastered bone white, its surface broken only by a panel door that led to the headmaster's office. In front of us was a proscenium stage, hung with velvet curtains so dark and deep a blue that to stare at them was like looking up and into a night sky without stars. At either end of the stage stood lecterns like church towers without steeples, waiting to be crowned by whatever master or senior boy rose to take his place behind them. Beside one lectern stood an American flag in a stanchion tipped with an eagle; on the wall beside the other hung a polished oak plaque, taller than a man, into which had been set framed and captioned photographs of all the boys from our school who had died in the Second War, sepia-toned pictures 3

of aviators in the cockpits of their Hellcats, faded en-
largements of Army lieutenants standing beside their
tents, studio portraits of stern young Navy officers
dressed in their whites.

The organ sounded a chord and we rose; the organ
sounded another chord and we sang. "Noble hymns set
to music of virtue, specially edited for private schools,"
were what we sang. There were hymns for Christmas
and Thanksgiving, hymns for the birthdays of Presidents, hymns to send boys marching off to classes in
the morning or marching back to their rooms at night.
I was six when I entered the school; I was almost eighteen when I left it. I began singing hymns in the chapel
the same year I was bar mitzvahed. The school called
itself nonsectarian. That meant: if Jews wanted to send
their sons to it, the school would treat them like everyone else. But since everyone else wasn't Jewish, that
meant that when boys turned thirteen Jews and Gentiles
alike went to chapel, and when the organ sounded,
everyone stood and sang.

Most of the hymns had words that were impossible
to pronounce. It wasn't that "Fairest Lord Jesus" or
"For All the Saints" were written in a language other
than English, but for a thirteen-year-old boy about to
be called to the Torah, "How sweet the name of Jesus
sounds" was blasphemous. All around me, boys stood
and sang, thinking about everything except what they
were saying or thinking about nothing except when they
could sit down. Not me. I stood and sweated and studied
the text, picking and choosing when to give voice and
when to pretend. If the other boys found out what I was
doing, they'd call me a kike. If God found out, He'd
burn me to a crisp. Whenever a hymn was posted that
had no forbidden words, I felt relieved and sang it loud
and clear. Now and then, though, a hymn was posted
that wasn't just safe to say but beautiful. Then, what I
felt was more than relief. Then, when the organ
4   sounded, my heart rose with it.

One morning, the signboard next to the flag read "Hymn 198." I turned to it and scanned it before the organ began. The text had one problem, but only one, a single reference in its first verse to "God's new Messiah." The entire third verse looked like a disaster, full of "burning martyrs," "Jesus' bleeding feet," Calvaries and crosses, but the signboard read only "1 and 2," so I felt safe. The organ sounded and we rose. "Once to every man and nation" it began. The music rolled out above us, harps and trumpets, triplets and bass chords. "Comes th-e moment t-o de-cide, In th-e strife of truth with falsehood, For th-e good or ev-il side." Thirty years later, it's difficult to know why what happened next happened. Maybe it was the harps and the trumpets; maybe it was the minor key of the piece; maybe it was the poignancy of the Welsh melody. Maybe it was all that, and certainly it was the words, but that hymn went into my heart like a wedge into green wood. "Some gre-at cause, God's new Messiah, Of-f'ring ea-ch the bloom o-r blight, and th-e choice goes by for-ev-er, 'Twixt th-at dark-ness and that light." Maybe those were the perfect words set to the perfect tune for a boy who felt trapped—a boy who wanted to please God but was afraid of others, a boy who wanted to please others but was afraid of God. I wanted to choose between truth and falsehood; I wanted to choose between bloom and blight. I wanted to decide but I couldn't; I wanted to act but I was afraid. Instead I kept singing. "Then t-o side with truth i-s no-ble When w-e share her wretch-ed crust." The music drove the words. "Ere he-r cause bring fame an-d pro-fit, And 'tis prosperous to be just." The music kept playing; the wedge sank deeper. "Then i-t is the brave ma-n chooses, While th-e cow-ard stands a-side." That's when the wedge sank half its length and stayed there. That's when this book actually began. It's been thirty years and still I don't know how brave men choose between darkness and light.

Every time we sang Hymn 198, it tapped the wedge, but drove it no deeper. Then, when I turned fifteen, the school's headmaster found a hammer of his own. The headmaster was named Mr. Hallowell, John Hallowell. He was about seven feet tall and looked like Abraham Lincoln, stooped, careworn, and lined. Every time he spoke to us in chapel, we expected the Gettysburg Address. He spoke haltingly, with many grave hmms and huhs while he paused, not so much to search for words as to reflect on them. A simple admonition about courtesy during meals came out as troubled as Kierkegaard's *Either-Or*. The only class he taught was a seminar entitled *Philosophy and Religion*. It was an honors class, open only to seniors, but once a year the headmaster selected a philosophical topic for an essay contest required of all underclassmen. I forget, now, what the prizes were, perhaps copies of Nietzsche's *Genealogy of Morals*, maybe nothing more than notes on the headmaster's letterhead inviting the winners to join his seminar their senior years. Everyone looked forward to the contest as much as they did to trips to the infirmary, but it was that contest that took up where Hymn 198 had left off.

One warm and fragrant afternoon in May, sixty of us filed into the study hall, found our desks, removed our jackets, loosened our ties, and waited while blue books were distributed and the headmaster's secretary, an old maid who had once taught third grade, wrote the topic on the board. "Some men are born great," she wrote in symmetrical longhand. "Some men achieve greatness," she continued, yellow chalk on a green board. "Some men have greatness thrust upon them." She turned and faced us, gray glasses, a starched blouse, and a black skirt. "That is your topic," she said, her voice like a line drawn with a ruler. "You are to take a position, agree or disagree, attack and defend, using specific examples based on your knowledge of history. You have two hours." She turned and left us alone on

6

our honor. Did she say knowledge of history? What knowledge? Someone groaned. Outside, the elms had just leafed out. The air smelled of cut grass and daffodils. What great men? We looked at each other, then out the windows. Had she said two hours? Not one of us knew enough to fill twenty minutes. Alexander the Great, I'd studied. Disraeli, I'd read about. Churchill, I'd heard of. Spengler's Great Man riding the back of History like a flea on an elephant; Hegel's Great Man as nothing but a ventriloquist's dummy; Marx's Great Man as a stick that one class used to beat another—no one even mentioned such things in my presence for another ten years. The boundaries between nature and nurture, the line between fate and free will—none of this I understand even now. To have asked a roomful of teenage boys to address such topics was like asking ants to be eagles. Some of us had just stopped wetting our beds; some of us still hadn't discovered how to masturbate. Not one of us had become a self. Not one of us was close to being a man, let alone a great one. I tried to answer the headmaster's questions, but all I discovered was my own ignorance. The space I thought was full was empty, and into it the wedge sank deeper.

No one seemed to notice what was sticking out of my chest. Every time I rolled over in bed, I felt it; every time I buttoned my shirt, I touched it. Morning and night, I wondered: why are some people brave and some people cowards, why do some stand up and others turn away, why do some people do good and others evil? Why and how, inhale and exhale, the wedge heaved in my chest. Finally, when I was sixteen, someone noticed. Her name was Mrs. Roundee. She was a ravaged old bluestocking English teacher who smelled like an ashtray. Her solution to my problem came from a Western movie: The hero lies on his back with an arrow in his leg. His sidekick kneels beside him. "Jimmy, Jimmy!" says the sidekick. "Pull it out, Wes," says the hero. Wes tries but it's too deep. "It won't budge, Jimmy!" "Then 7

break it off, goddamnit, and push it though." "O.K.,"
says Wes. He snaps the shaft and pushes. Jimmy
screams and passes out. When he wakes up, he's in bed,
safe and sound, back at the fort. What Mrs. Roundee
did was assign us to read *The Bridge of San Luis Rey*.

Thirty years later, *The Bridge* is probably dismissed
as a cliché, if it's remembered at all. It's about a little
monk named Brother Juniper who stops to rest, one
day, on the side of a mountain in Peru. While he's
standing there, catching his breath, looking across the
distance, he can see, way off, the rope bridge that links
Cuzco to Lima. The year is 1714 and the bridge is
already hundreds of years old. Far off, he sees it, and
as he looks, he hears the faintest noise and then he sees
the bridge snap and five little figures fall into the gorge
below. It is then that he decides to spend the rest of his
life trying to discover why—if God controls the fate of
the world and all who live in it—those five particular
people happened to be on the bridge when it broke. To
do this he inquires into their lives to trace their paths
backwards, not just from the minute to the hour to the
day of their deaths, but back beyond that, through all
the days and months and years that formed a pattern
whose meaning was hidden until they fell to their
deaths. For his troubles, Brother Juniper is burned at
the stake.

That book finished off what Hymn 198 had begun.
Mrs. Roundee's solution was to push the wedge all the
way in so that, like the arrow in the movie, it could be
pulled out the other side. The people in *The Bridge*
made choices and suffered their fates or, as the hymn
said, "share[d] her wretched crust." *The Bridge* asked
how people came to deserve their destinies and offered
a way to find the answer; I was old enough to understand
the book's questions, just as I'd understood the headmaster's and the hymn's. But I wasn't old enough to
8   know how to answer them. The book pounded the ques-

tions all the way into me, but nothing came out the other side except the tip of another book—in fact, the tip of this one. I'm forty-five now, old enough to play Brother Juniper. Old enough to reach around and pull the wedge or the arrow or the stake or whatever it is out of my own back. Old enough to answer the questions I've been asking myself since I was thirteen.

I decided to do this by inquiring into the motives of heroes. Heroes defined as human beings who choose to risk their own lives to save others. Heroes as rescuers. Heroism defined as altruism accompanied by extreme jeopardy. The act of rescue as a choice made either once or again and again, but a choice that transforms the rescuer as if he were a man stepping out of the shadows into the light. Long before Hymn 198 was written, there were rabbis who said, "The world is a spinning die and everything turns and changes, man is turned into an angel and angel into man, and the head into the foot and the foot into the head. Thus all things change . . . the topmost to the undermost and the undermost to the topmost." The instant before a heroic act, a man is a man; an instant later, he looks like an angel; a few minutes more and he looks like a man again.

This book is about such transformations. For a year, I traveled back and forth across the United States talking and listening to people who had risked their lives for the sake of others. I asked them why they did what they did. I talked to rich and poor, black and white, Northern and Southern, women and men. The shortest interview I conducted lasted a day; the longest went on, inter-mittently, for two months. What follow are the stories nine people told me about themselves and their motives.

Their stories are full of contradictions. In them, fools become wise and cowards become brave. Again and again, vice becomes virtue and weakness breeds strength. I hadn't expected to hear this. At first, I dismissed it. But paradoxes are powerful constructions; 9

wound within them, spiraled inside them, are forces as powerful as anything in nature. The energies these forces hold and are held by are like the energies at the center of atoms. The lives that follow and the contradictions at their centers may seem, at first, as common as water or air, but the energy in them, once released, is enough to turn night into day. What follows are nine stories of such release.

ACTION HEROES

Soldiers

I WAS FIVE when the Korean War began and eight when it ended. It was the first war I'd ever seen. I watched it on television every afternoon. First came the puppet shows, then the fighting. Kukla, Fran, and Ollie, then Starfighters, Sabre jets, and General MacArthur. Clouds of flame cascaded down valleys. "Jellied gasoline," the announcer said. I looked at my toast: it had apple jelly on it. I walked into the kitchen and held up my plate. "How do you make jelly explode?" I asked my mother. When I was old enough, I bought comic books with chromo covers of GIs, thin as knives, holding their rifles like spears, charging Commies with yellow faces.

There were 131 Medals of Honor issued during the Korean War. Ninety-four of them were posthumous. Of the men who lived to receive their medals, thirty-one are alive today. I spoke with ten of them, and interviewed four; two of these interviews follow. I chose to speak with such survivors for two reasons: first, because the Korean War, its pictures and stories, real and otherwise, defined my earliest understanding of what heroes did in battle; and second, because the events of 13 that war happened so long ago. The war in Vietnam is still being fought. In books, on television, and in the movies, this war continues. Survivors weep; widows grieve; partisans, for and against, still exchange accusations. The Vietnam War won't be over for another ten years. But the Korean War is finished. No one debates, anymore, its miseries, stupidities, triumphs, and ordeals. The passage of time has changed it—as it changes every war—into an archeological ruin as capable of revealing certain truths about the human condition as a city found buried in the sand.

Recipients of the Medal of Honor don't like to be called winners. "It's not a contest," they say. There are stringent requirements, though. Everyone is familiar with the rule about "risk of life, above and beyond the call of duty." But that risk must be confirmed by at least two eyewitnesses; their testimony must be seconded by the recommendations of superior officers, and those recommendations must survive the scrutiny of a whole chain of command that can veto a nomination long before it reaches the desk of the President. I mention all this because some of the acts to be described in this chapter are so extraordinary that anyone might doubt them, were it not for the standards of proof the military imposes on itself.

Time has trimmed details from the stories told by Ronald Rosser (Master Sergeant, U.S. Army, retired) and Gerry Murphy (Captain, U.S. Marines, retired), turning what may once have been loose bundles of fact into neatly wrapped narrative packages that sometimes sound like stories from a *Weekly Reader* and sometimes like episodes from a war comic. Rosser, in fact, showed me an ancient blood-and-guts paperback that featured his story and spoke of long-ago movie deals that had never worked out. Murphy, on the other hand, said he'd never spoken to any outsider, not a single journalist, 14   producer, or writer, since he'd done what he'd done.

The style of each man's narrative, the way he spoke and what he did and didn't say, was markedly different. Rosser had evidently told his story many times, not just because he liked to talk about himself, but because he was a wonderful storyteller. Sitting in the half light of his little living room, in his tiny house, in the winter, in Ohio, rocking in his La-Z-Boy, rhythmically beating the arm of his chair at every point of impact, dramatic and ballistic, in his story, he reenacted what he'd done, and reproduced what he'd heard and seen as if it were all part of a basketball game he'd played yesterday and not a war he'd fought nearly forty years ago. Murphy, however, seemed to remember nearly nothing. He sat facing me, at a table, by the window of my motel room in New Mexico, shifting now and then to relieve his back, but speaking with few gestures and little emphasis, his manner as flat as the landscape that surrounded us. Trying to recall exactly what had happened, he spoke in the amazed voice of a sleepwalker who'd just come awake, standing by the side of some railroad tracks, his face a few feet from the cars that roared past him. Asked why he'd done what he'd done, he answered with a blank shrug; pressed to respond to the idea that he may have acted out of self-preservation, he looked honestly surprised. His reticence was equal to Rosser's explicitness; his modesty was matched by Rosser's boastfulness: both were camouflages that revealed as much as they hid.

I

Rosser was twenty-two when he'd done what he'd done. He had the arms, back, and belly of a weight lifter, the legs of a football player, and the stamina of a long-distance runner—attributes inherited, but further developed by working eight hours a day, in the low-ceilinged "rooms" of a coal mine in Ohio. His military assignment—a volunteer assignment—was radio operator, a job said to require a forty-inch chest and a four-inch hat size—a job for men strong enough to carry a hundred pounds of radio equipment on their backs in addition to their own rations, ammunition, and weapons, but also a job for men dumb enough to do it, since carrying a radio, sprouted with aerials, was like carrying a sign with ten-foot letters that said "SHOOT ME." The lives of most radio operators could be counted in days or weeks; Rosser had lasted seven months. One explanation for this can be found in his nickname: his friends called him "Gunslinger." As a child, he'd hunted with a .22 and, later, with a .410 shotgun. During his first enlistment, he'd been well trained by veterans of the Second War, then assigned to a weapons-testing company that spent its time on a range, firing small-arms prototypes. After he'd reenlisted in 1951, he spent his days—while everyone else rested, trying to recover from nights of attack and counterattack—practicing with his carbine, a light weapon usually carried by officers that could fire a thirty-round clip when set on automatic.

Rosser was part of a zero-sum game, being played out at twenty degrees below zero in a valley in north-central Korea, an area called the Iron Triangle, a place of stalemate where both sides took turns attacking and defending entrenched positions in a war of attrition similar to the bloodletting practiced in Europe thirty-five years earlier. In the second week of January 1952, Rosser served as a radio operator for a forward artillery observer, both attached to a reinforced company of 173 men sent against a heavily fortified Chinese hill position. That network of bunkers and trenches had already withstood attacks by a reinforced platoon and one other reinforced company. Both had been obliterated in successive assaults against the Chinese conducted during the winter of 1951. The American counterposition was a long ridge, its point tipped by a Browning automatic rifle post, a mile and a half from the Chinese hill.

16

Rosser's company stepped off to attack at 3 a.m. Even before they were outside their own wire, they'd lost a man to frostbite. By the time they passed their forward post and started down the slope of their ridge, the sun had risen. Above them, they could see the Chinese, racing along their own ridgelines, repositioning their heavy machine guns, dragging their 76mm cannons, keeping up with them, tracking them. A half mile ahead, their lead platoon walked into an ambush. One soldier made it back. "They're all dead, Captain," he said, "they're all dead." By the time the company was a mile outside its lines, its sergeants and all its lieutenants but one were dead, and its captain had been severely wounded, his face sliced open, ear to ear, by a piece of shrapnel. Many of the men who could still walk were bleeding themselves out into the snow. From all sides, they were being hit by artillery, automatic-weapons, and small-arms fire. Rosser hadn't been touched. He radioed his regimental commander, a colonel. He gave his name and rank and reported his company's losses. The colonel asked to speak to Rosser's captain. Rosser crawled across to him, and held the handset to the captain's ear, listening, since the man could barely speak and had begun to lose track of the action. "Captain," Rosser heard the colonel say. "Yes, sir," mumbled the captain. "How many men do you have left?" asked the colonel. "Thirty-five, sir," answered the captain. "Captain," said the colonel, "I want you to assemble your men and assault your objective. That's an order, Captain." The captain couldn't move his lips by then. But his eyes—his eyes were intact. Rosser looked at them and what he saw was shock and amazement. Rosser broke radio contact, put down the handset, and what he said was: "I'll go, Captain. I'll do it."

All the men who couldn't walk but could still fire their weapons, Rosser arranged in two groups, one at either end of an arc. These men he told to fire to protect his flanks. Those who could still move, he assembled. 17

"O.K.," he said, "we're going up the hill. Everyone's gonna key in on me. You do what I do. We're gonna lay down fire on those bastards and run right over 'em. Step off at my signal."

They drew themselves up; he gave a yell, and ran. He ran faster than he'd ever run. He heard Thompsons firing on his flanks. He ran and ran, through the snow, in the cold, up the hill. Three feet from the first Chinese trenches, he threw himself down and looked back to see who'd made it. He was all alone. Some had been killed; some had been wounded; some had been too frightened to follow. He was alone.

He lay on his belly, in front of the trench, separated from the men in it by a dirt parapet. He was so close, he could hear them talking. He wanted to run, but he stopped himself. If he ran, they'd shoot him in the back. He was certain of that. He was also certain that, no matter what he did, he was a dead man. He held his breath and listened: he heard three voices. Those were the odds. He gathered his strength and then, with a tremendous yell, he leapt up and straddled the trench.

At this point in his storytelling, Rosser sprang up, out of his La-Z-Boy, onto the balls of his feet. Sixty years old, strong and thick, he stood in front of me, knees flexed, head down, legs apart, eyes moving, his carbine pointed at the men below him. He'd been wrong about the odds. There were eight of them—six kneeling in a row, their rifles butt-down on the ground. The seventh stood in front of him, "close enough to piss on," surprised, looking up at him. Behind Rosser stood the eighth. Rosser couldn't see him, but he would feel the muzzle of the man's rifle creeping up the small of his back. As I watched, Rosser dropped to a half crouch, put his carbine in the ear of the man in front of him, and shot him in the head. The top and sides of the man's skull blew out like a balloon. Then Rosser swiveled and shot the man behind him, first in the throat, but the man didn't drop, so he shot him through the heart. He thumbed his carbine to automatic then, and showed me what he did next. Imagine a man fly-fishing, casting for trout, his arm bent back at the elbow, then flexed, in an arc, up and out. Then, as you picture that, turn the rod into a whip and watch the man snap it back with his wrist, his forearm flexed again, but now rising up and back toward his shoulder. Think of such a fluid arc, the rod become a whip, the forearm and the wrist sending a line down, out, and then up, and—as the line rises up and back—imagine Rosser gracefully moving his carbine set on automatic, placing a line straight up the center of that row of six kneeling men.

He killed them all. He had a single white-phosphorus grenade with him. He bounded across the trench to a bunker, knelt on its roof, and gently, with two fingers, like a man stroking the chin of a cat, he rolled in the grenade. Two men, on fire, ran out, screaming. He shot them. Everywhere, there were Chinese. The trench he'd cleared, the bunker he'd blown, were part of a network. A Chinese pitched a grenade at him. Rosser saw it coming and dove behind the body of a dead man. The corpse took the blast; a soldier popped up; Rosser shot him in the head. All this, in seconds.

He swerved down a connecting trench and saw, at the far end, a file of soldiers running at him, full tilt, led by a man with a submachine gun who opened fire as soon as Rosser saw him. Rosser had known he was a dead man from the moment he'd looked back and seen he was alone, so, instead of turning, he put his head down and charged, firing as he ran, ducking, weaving, and bouncing off the trench walls, his coat flapping around him, feeling the rounds buzz by his head, feeling the rounds burn through his coat, Rosser and the Chinese, both firing and missing, headed for each other like trains in a tunnel. What happened, though, was that the Chinese emptied his magazine before Rosser did, and as the Chinese broke stride to rearm, the men behind him kept coming. They collided 19 with him, but Rosser never stopped; the submachine gunner panicked and turned; the men behind him panicked and turned; Rosser kept coming. For a few seconds he chased them down the trench, but then he stopped, replaced his banana clip, braced himself, thumbed his carbine to semiautomatic, took aim, and began to kill the men, one by one, like a knocker killing cattle in a chute. First the submachine gunner, who'd become last in line, then the one in front, and the one in front of him, a head shot, a neck shot, a back shot; a head shot, a neck shot, a back shot, he killed them all.

By then, he was out of grenades and low on ammunition. He found his way back to the first trench and climbed out. Standing in front of him was a single American, a young soldier who'd made it up the slope long after Rosser had disappeared into the trenches. Just as he and Rosser saw each other, a burst of heavy machine-gun fire turned the man's arm into a bloody pulp. Rosser picked him up, slung him over his shoulder, and started down the hill, crunching through the snow. The Chinese kept after him, with machine guns, small arms, and grenades. Rosser wasn't touched. He began to laugh, long, loud, and happy, a dead man enjoying the joke of being alive. At the bottom of the slope, he came upon the company's lone surviving lieutenant, who'd dropped to his knees, firing his carbine to cover Rosser's retreat. As Rosser came even with him, the man rose to his feet. Rosser stopped and there they stood, bullets whizzing through the air, Rosser grinning like a jack-o'-lantern, the wounded man slung over his shoulder, the lieutenant resting his weapon in the snow. "What's your name, Private?" said the lieutenant. "Do you know what you've done?" "I sure do," said Rosser, still grinning. "But do you really know what you've done?" repeated the lieutenant. "I sure as shit do," answered Rosser, as happy as he'd ever been. "Then," said the lieutenant, "I want to shake your hand." Rosser rested his carbine against his leg and the two men shook. "Congratulations," said the lieutenant. "Thank you, sir," said Rosser, the two of them like soldiers at a ceremony.

Rosser laid the wounded man next to his captain, put a tourniquet on him, collected as many grenades and thirty-round clips as he could carry, and went back up the hill. On the ridgeline above him, he could see a Chinese cannon crew furiously cranking their weapon, traversing its barrel, lowering its sights, trying to blow a hole through him with a shell meant to kill a tank. Rosser heard the report and felt the air blast as the first projectile flew past, then heard another and another, and as each round blew a hole in the snow, he laughed, giddy, yelling at the Chinese, "You missed! You missed! You missed me, you son of a bitch!"

The trench he'd cleared was occupied again, soldiers standing behind the parapet, firing at him as he trudged toward them, his carbine in one hand, a grenade in the other. At the outside of his range he lofted the grenade, and, as it peaked, the Chinese stopped and watched it fall between them, its trajectory as perfect as a mortar round. As soon as the grenade exploded, Rosser broke into a run, leaped the trench, pivoted, pitched another grenade behind him just to be sure, pulled the pins from two more, tossed them, on the run, into a bunker, and kept going as its roof blew out behind him. He felt happy again, light and gay. Anything that moved, he fired at and hit, a helmet, a hat, a padded jacket, he pointed and shot, emptying clip after clip, not laughing anymore, but so elated, he outran a machine-gun burst, diving behind a tiny rise, just high enough to shield him as the bullets dug up the snow where he'd been.

Once more he walked down the hill and once more he collected grenades and ammunition, but this time when he climbed the slope, there were more Chinese waiting for him and he knew they'd kill him. He only came close enough to throw grenades, then he with-   21 drew. By then, a unit of soldiers and stretcher bearers had reached his company. There were ninety dead. Rosser made several trips back and forth to evacuate the wounded. News, official and unofficial, of what he'd done traveled fast. Within a week, there were photos of him in all the American newspapers. He handed me a Xerox of one. It showed him cutting notches in the stock of a carbine. "Counting the Score" was its caption. "Pfc. Ronald Rosser," it read, "notches carbine to indicate 13 Reds he killed in a single engagement. Pfc. Rosser, up for Medal of Honor, says he did it to avenge his brother killed in Korean fighting."

That's the explanation, then; he did it all to get even: the Reds killed his kid brother and the rest came naturally. The peculiar thing is that, forty years later, he can remember many of the men he killed, but he can't remember very much about his brother. He can remember his brother's name, which was Richard. He can remember when Richard enlisted, where he fought, when, where, and how he was wounded, and when, where, and how he was killed, but he can't remember much about who Richard was or what the two of them, older brother and younger brother, did together long before Richard died in battle. Richard seems to have been engulfed by the war, like a house in the path of a lava flow. Rosser claims he did it all out of love—killed the men in the trench, killed the men from the bunker, killed the file of soldiers, and killed many more before— all because of love. Of course, it may have started that way and then changed, like a solid into a gas, love transformed, love vaporized, incandescent, love into hate. But that doesn't explain his power, his laughter, or the epic deeds he did. He moved, untouched, in battle, like a man protected by a god and possessed by demons.

No one yet understands the physics and chemistry of such primal emotions as love and hate. Perhaps the transformation of the one into the other did release an

22

energy that both propelled Rosser and protected him. The question remains: how did such a process occur? If love began the reaction and hate ended it, what happened in between? What if hate were not an end product, but a by-product, an intermediate, volatile emotion, itself transformed into yet another state of being, neither pure love nor pure hate, but a powerful amalgam, yet to be described?

What follows, then, is an investigation into that process of transformation, a process that caused a man to act in ways both more and less than human.

Rosser was the second-born of seventeen children. First-born was a girl, then Rosser, then another girl, then Richard, the brother who died. Rosser's mother bore and raised children for nineteen years. Rosser's father began as a coal miner, but rose to the rank of superintendent of what was then the largest mechanized mine in the world. Rosser became the family protector. How and why that happened, he didn't explain, but "if anyone messed with anyone in the family, they had to answer to me," he said. "If someone did something, they knew I'd be after 'em. They knew I'd fight 'em. It didn't make no difference how long it took to make things right, ten years, it didn't matter, I had the time. One day or another, I'd even the score. People knew: 'Ron never forgets.' "

That's how it began, then: an oldest son, a family protector, a kid who held grudges, a kid who liked to fight. By the time he was in high school, Rosser had probably taken on everyone of any consequence in town. The North Koreans should have known better than to kill his brother. The actual progress of events was as follows: Ron, age seventeen, enlisted in the Army. In July 1949, his enlistment ended. One month later, Richard enlisted. Ron went to work in a coal mine. In February 1951, the North Koreans killed Richard. Three months later, Ron reenlisted.

The Army wanted to send him to Germany, but Rosser told them he'd go AWOL. "You can put me in the stockade, but I'll go over the wall. I'm combat infantry, goddamnit. Send me to Korea." No one, absolutely no one *wanted* to go to Korea. In October 1950, the Chinese had come south, in force. At the Chosin reservoir, they'd nearly had the Marines for Thanksgiving dinner. In April 1951, MacArthur had been cashiered. The war settled into a stalemate, airpower and artillery against manpower, neither side able to overwhelm the other. U.S. military and strategic planners worried that a Soviet invasion of Europe might be next. That may have been why the Army wanted to send someone trained like Rosser to Germany. Rosser had a score to settle, though. By June, he was in Japan.

There, he made choices, voluntary choices, that he hoped would let him live long enough to kill as many people as possible. Asked to choose between intelligence reconnaissance and heavy mortars, he chose the mortars. Both were combat assignments, but one was more exposed than the other. Not that there was any safe place to be: of the one hundred men who volunteered with Rosser for combat, only seven were alive ten months later.

Once he reached the front, Rosser lost all hope of living long enough to avenge his brother. In his first week, two events made him understand he was as good as dead: on his first day in combat, his mortar squad came under heavy artillery bombardment. To escape the shelling, Rosser dived into an abandoned North Korean bunker. Too late, he discovered it had been used as a latrine. "Talk about 'Welcome to a World of Shit,' " he said. Three days later, walking single file, the man in front of him was shot by a sniper. Rosser froze in his tracks: the sniper's cross hairs had swung across him on their way to the man three steps ahead. "That's when I knew. Next time, any time, it could be me," he said.

One day, an artillery forward observer walked uninvited into Rosser's squad bunker. He looked at each man and then announced that he'd just lost his third radio operator in three days and needed a new one. "O.K., girls, who wants to volunteer?" he asked. No one said a word. "Chickenshits," said the forward observer. "Chickenshit cowards," he continued. He was just getting warmed up when Rosser stopped him. "Shut up," said Rosser. "You got no right to call people cowards just 'cause they don't want to get shot. You're asking people to volunteer to get killed." The forward observer looked at Rosser and took his time answering. "You!" he said. "You're the biggest chickenshit in the bunch." Rosser glared at him. "All right, Corporal. You got your volunteer. Now *shut up*!"

Rosser was (and is) a passionate but not a stupid man. He knew he was volunteering to die. Why did he do it? He liked to fight; he knew how to fight; he'd volunteered to fight. He wasn't about to let anyone call him a coward. Granted all that—why did he volunteer for an assignment that was sure to get him killed? Did he think he'd survive? The answer to that is: No. By the end of his first week in combat, he knew he was living on borrowed time. Why, then, did he volunteer? My guess is that he wanted to "even the score." There are three ways to do that: seek revenge, make atonement, or do both. The *only* thing Rosser said about his childhood was that he was the family protector. "Protector" was his word. He'd failed to protect Richard. Rage and guilt were the consequences: rage at Richard's killers, guilt and rage at himself. If he could punish himself *and* punish others, if he could kill *and* die, then the score would be perfectly even.

It didn't work out that way. Instead of dying, he lived. Rosser and his forward observer formed a team that outlived rifle company after rifle company. They'd be assigned to one; it would assault a position; they'd move forward with it, calling in artillery, fighting as it fought—but, in the end, they'd be the only ones left 25 alive. They began to get reputations: Flying Dutchmen, Typhoid Marys, the ones who lived while everyone else died. Imagine the effect of such a "charmed" life on a man like Rosser: he'd already survived a brother. His role, as radio operator, was to help his forward observer help the artillery to help the men assaulting the enemy. In spite of everything Rosser did, the men around him died. One hundred and fifty at a time. Time after time. Once, moving up a blasted hill, dodging from tree to ruined tree, he felt the hair on the back of his neck stand up. He looked around like a man startled by a loud noise. Then he saw it: the ghost of a man, his head hanging from a branch, connected to a huge, flapping tent of skin, blown into the side of the tree by the same explosion that had blown the man's body out of its very skin. It was as if Rosser had been cursed, marooned on an island of ghosts—his only power, the power to kill; his only escape, finding his own death.

He began to take pleasure in killing. In hand-to-hand combat, a North Korean charged him; Rosser lowered his carbine, braced it, and let the man run onto his bayonet. Face to face with him, Rosser smelled the garlic on his breath and watched the life drain from his eyes. He began to play an awful game: again and again, he'd trap a man and wait for him to beg for mercy. He'd lower his weapon and watch the man's eyes fill with hope. Then, as they did, he'd shoot the man in the head. Over and over he did this. Forty years later, he isn't proud of it, but, he says, "Don't get me wrong. A lot of guys did stuff like that, cruel stuff, but they did it because they were scared. But me, I did it because I hated those bastards."

One day, in the fall of the year, he stood on a hilltop and watched, through binoculars, a rifle company assault a nearby Chinese hill position. He watched the company charge straight into a wall of concussion grenades and automatic-weapons fire. He watched the survivors fall back. Then he saw a single man rise from the ranks and charge, all alone, up the hill, throwing grenades as he ran, advancing behind their explosions until, finally, he reached the crest and disappeared. Then, as Rosser watched, he saw the men who had stayed behind rise as one man and, as one man, he saw them draw their bayonets from their scabbards and, as one man, he watched them upend and fix them. Across the distance, he heard the faint scrape, slide, and lock of hafts to muzzles, and then, louder, across the distance, he heard the shouts and saw the charge, a line of men moving like one man, swiftly rushing up the slope, taking the summit, and sweeping it clean. All this he watched and later he remembered that one man.

By winter, Rosser and his forward observer had been absorbed by a company occupying a ridge opposite a hill the Chinese had turned into a network of bunkers and revetments, crisscrossed with trenches. The Americans sent out patrols at night, but they never came back. Instead, the Chinese came, night after night. On one of those nights, Rosser was alone in a foxhole when he heard a plucked twang, the sound ice-cold barbed wire made when whoever lifted it to climb through had let it go. It was so dark, Rosser couldn't see his hand in front of his face, and so cold his spit thickened in midair. He stacked a pile of grenades in front of him and waited. Maybe he was nervous or maybe he was frightened, but whatever he was, his legs began to twitch, then they began to jerk, then they started jumping. He ground the butt of his carbine into his foot to keep it still. Then he heard a sound he'd never heard before: someone nearby was pounding a drum; it was sure to reveal his position. He looked around, frantic, trying to locate the noise, so he could stop it. Then he realized—the pounding was coming from him. It was his own heart. He pressed his chest to stop it. He could hear footsteps in the snow. He started rolling grenades out in front of him. Bodies started blowing through the air. A machine gun next to him and a BAR in front of 27 him opened fire. He kept rolling grenades. Rolling and throwing them. In the morning, the snow was covered with blood, but there wasn't a single body.

A few weeks passed. Rosser and his forward observer were ordered to accompany a reinforced platoon of seventy-three men, sent out, at night, "to maintain the initiative." The Chinese let them through their lines, then encircled them. Rosser's forward observer was wounded by shrapnel, his calf cut clean through. Rosser lifted him onto his back. There were nine men left who could walk. Rosser led them out, breaking through the ice of a frozen stream, wading through the freezing water, his buddy on his back. The Chinese ran along the bank, firing burp guns and throwing grenades, trying to kill every last one of them. Behind them as they fled, Rosser and the others could hear the Chinese killing the wounded. "Korea was nothing but a slaughter," Rosser said, "and I was on both sides of it."

His forward observer was still in the hospital when a shell hit Rosser's squad bunker and buried Rosser alive. He was dug out, still breathing, but the experience reminded him: he'd survived too many disasters; his days were numbered. He began to train his replacement. "You want to live," Rosser told him, "you listen to me." A reinforced company was sent to flank the Chinese hill whose garrison had destroyed the reinforced platoon. The company never returned. Plans were made to send another; the company chosen was the one to which Rosser was attached. Twelve hours before the attack, Rosser sat in the company mess, drinking coffee. The man he'd trained to replace him, the man who'd serve as radio operator for the upcoming assault, walked in and sat down next to him. Rosser nodded hello. The man nodded back. They sat side by side, drinking coffee. Then Rosser turned to speak and saw that the man was weeping. "Huge, goddamn tears," Rosser said. Rosser finished his coffee and went to see his captain. He volunteered to take the man's place. "No way he could do

28

his job," Rosser said. "He was cracking up just drinking his coffee. Someone had to go. Those guys needed all the help they could get. I was the best man. I'd done it a million times."

Rosser knew he was volunteering to die. He knew it then as he'd known it when he'd volunteered the first time to serve the corporal he later saved, carrying him on his back across that frozen stream. Rosser claimed he volunteered the second time out of pride and experience: he was the best; he'd done it "a million times." But what had he done those million times? What he'd done was live when he should have died, lived even though everyone around him perished. Again and again, again and again. Richard had died. The rifle companies had died. The reinforced platoon had died. Rosser kept living. From the outside looking in, his survival was a blessing. From the inside looking out, it was a curse. Of course, he'd killed many men. He'd grown cruel and murderous. But no matter how many he killed, he couldn't bring his brother or anyone else back to life. Revenge *and* atonement were the way to even the score. But he hadn't atoned. He kept trying, but he was just too lucky. It was as if he had a mark on his forehead. He was cursed to live and see others die. That's why he kept volunteering while God or Fate or the Devil kept him alive. The longer he stayed alive, the more tormented he became. The more tormented and the more cruel and the more compassionate: by volunteering, he saved the weeping man; by volunteering, he tried to protect the rifle company he served.

Of course, that did no good. Ninety men died and Rosser survived without a scratch. Which brought him to the moment when he volunteered a third time, the moment after the colonel ordered the captain to assault his objective and the captain's eyes registered dumb shock. This is how Rosser explained it: "The captain couldn't do it. I was experienced. I'd been through a hundred fights. I knew we were all going to die. Every- 29 one was going to die. I knew that. But I couldn't see myself living to watch those other guys die before me. I couldn't have lived with myself. I had to do it for them. I couldn't have lived. I couldn't have stood there and watched them die."

He did it, then, because he couldn't bear to live to see another group of men—fellow soldiers, brothers-in-arms—die. He wanted to die instead. The chemistry and physics of all that led beyond feelings of love and hate to a state of torment in which suicide, homicidal rage, and atonement mingled with brotherly love. Rosser had lived for months in that tormented condition, surrounded by ghosts, unable to die, and never, ever able to kill enough to restore to life those he loved or pitied. That torment was his power. In the end, his laughter was an epiphany: he realized he was free to live. In the end, the only dead man he resurrected was himself.

II

The war Gerry Murphy fought a year later was a little worse than Rosser's: the stalemate on the battlefield had become a stalemate at the conference table. Dwight Eisenhower had been elected President by pledging to bring the boys home, but the North Koreans at Panmunjom remained unimpressed. U.S. Eighth Army Command continued to do what it could to "maintain the initiative." One of its last and more lunatic efforts was a call for volunteers to assault something called Ungok Hill, the local equivalent of the Rock of Gibraltar. Gerry Murphy's captain, a man named Blanchard, who had entered the Corps as an enlisted man and risen through the ranks—a career type known to be so tough and wild as to be called a "Mustang"—volunteered his company, Second Lieutenant Murphy included, to assault Ungok in broad daylight. In January 1953, Murphy had just returned from R and R in Japan with only a month left in his tour of duty when he discovered what his captain had done.

Blanchard asked Murphy to volunteer to lead the assault, but Murphy refused: he was a short-timer, he'd risked his life by doing his duty many times before; he wanted to go home alive. Blanchard accepted his refusal and assigned him to lead the platoon that would evacuate the wounded and the dead. The night before the assault, Murphy went to mass and confession. Later he lay in his sleeping bag and said his rosary, sure he'd die and afraid of dying. "The whole idea was suicide; it was nothing but crazy. I couldn't understand how they could go through with it." At dawn, someone accidentally fired a round. "They'll cancel it now," he thought. "Surely they won't do it now." But they did. One hundred men in two platoons advanced across rice-paddy dikes to flank the hill. The North Koreans had mined the paddies and sighted in the dikes, but Marine Corsair aircraft strafed and bombed so fiercely that the platoons were able to reach the hill with enough men still alive to attack it. Murphy remembered seeing a Corsair, guns blazing, plow into the side of the hill, its pilot so fixated on his target that he'd forgotten to pull up.

After that, Murphy remembered seeing what was left of the assault units reach the top of the hill, the men silhouetted against the sky, milling about, every one of their officers but a sergeant killed, seventy men wounded, eighteen dead, the survivors shocked and leaderless. Until the day Murphy sat and spoke with me, that was the last thing he remembered until he came to his senses in a MASH unit, where a Navy doctor, who was picking shrapnel out of him, offended him by making a joke about the advantages of having a fat ass. For forty years, until I showed up in New Mexico, the Corsair's explosion and the Navy doctor's joke served as Murphy's only entrance and exit to a period of time that he knew had begun at dawn and ended at dusk but that he couldn't fully recall. With me sitting across from him, looking and listening, Murphy remembered more fully than, he said, he ever had—but his words and his voice were those of a man describing something he was seeing through binoculars, at extreme range, something whose scale and movement and very outline were conjectural.

The deeds of every Medal of Honor recipient are described in an official citation, and it is this citation, based on the testimony of eyewitnesses, that must serve as an armature for the bulk of Murphy's narrative. On the morning we met, Murphy remembered he'd jumped into a trench. There was a wounded man on a litter down there, he said. Other men stood above him. The litter had become stuck and the men above were too exhausted to think about how to free it. Murphy jumped in, told the wounded man to put his arms around his neck, ordered the other men to throw him a rope, and then told them to pull him and the wounded man up and out. Murphy's citation says that long before that, he had been "painfully wounded" by shrapnel. Later, in the MASH tent, with two spinals in him and the Navy doctor digging away, Murphy realized he had a hole in his left hand and shell fragments up and down the left side of his body. That was the first time he'd noticed this. The citation doesn't mention the trench, but does say that Murphy made several trips up and down the hill, supervising and "personally carrying many of the stricken Marines to safety." Then, the citation says, the enemy counterattacked and "during the ensuing battle, 2nd Lt. Murphy personally killed two of the enemy with his pistol." Murphy recollected he had a pistol, but he didn't remember using it, although he did recall he somehow lost it. In boot camp, Murphy had barely qualified on the rifle range, and to this day he doesn't own a weapon, doesn't hunt, and intensely distrusts the NRA. Nonetheless, his citation describes how, after he

32 killed the two men with his pistol, he used a carbine to

cover the retreat of his evacuation platoon and what was left of the two assault units, and that in spite of "intense pain from his previous wounds," he "seized an automatic rifle to provide more firepower." Murphy remembered using both the carbine and the BAR, but he couldn't recall how they came into his hands or how they left them.

After everyone reached the bottom of the hill, Murphy organized a final search party, went back up the hill, and found the bodies of four Marines. Evacuation of the wounded is, of course, common to all military services, foreign and domestic. Evacuation of the dead, no matter what the risk, is a Marine tradition, part of a code as old as the *Iliad*, embodied in the Corps's motto, "Semper Fidelis." The day we spoke, Murphy remembered something he'd forgotten for forty years. He wasn't sure how many trips it took to bring the bodies down, but he did recall dragging one down by its feet. Somehow, the man's pants came off and Murphy was mortified to see that the man was naked. "I was ashamed for him," Murphy said. "I was ashamed he had nothing on, no underwear, I mean, so he was naked for everyone to see. I felt bad for him." The next thing Murphy knew, he himself was in a medical tent, stripped of his clothes, listening to a surgeon make a coarse joke at his expense.

Blanchard recommended Murphy for the Medal of Honor, but Murphy didn't know that. What he did know was that, after a patrol a few months earlier, Blanchard had recommended him for the Silver Star. Murphy spent the next four months in and out of various hospitals. He was finally released in April, in San Francisco. There, in an awards ceremony at the Presidio, the commandant of the base presented Murphy with the Star and solicitously asked about his plans for the future. The commandant knew about the Medal, but Murphy still didn't, so Murphy dismissed the commandant's concern as noblesse oblige and told him he planned to   33 leave the service, go to New York, and study for a master's degree in education. It was there, one morning, sleeping off a hangover, that Murphy answered the phone and learned he was to receive the Medal of Honor. He was truly surprised.

Five years passed. Murphy earned his master's and found a job at a recreation center in a suburb of Boston. In 1958, the U.S. government interred an Unknown Soldier from the Korean War in Arlington Cemetery. Murphy and other Medal recipients were called to Washington to participate in the ceremony. They traveled in limousines in a slow cavalcade to the cemetery, along a route lined with soldiers from all the services. As Murphy looked out the window, he saw, unmistakably, the lone sergeant who had survived the assault on Ungok Hill. Murphy first told me the man's name was Hanes, but later in the day he corrected himself and changed it to Manes. He said he knew him because the man had served as Murphy's sergeant before transferring, for some reason Murphy didn't explain, to another platoon in the company. "Did you locate him after the ceremony?" I asked Murphy. "No," he said. "I never saw him again." "What about all those other people you rescued?" I asked. "Did you ever get in touch with them or did they ever get in touch with you? I mean, did you guys ever have some sort of reunion or anything like that?" "No," Murphy said, and left it at that. I tried to ask the question in another way. "Besides Manes," I asked, "what other noncoms and officers took part in the assault? Other lieutenants, other sergeants?" Murphy shrugged. "For the life of me," he said, "I don't even remember their names."

Murphy worked in Boston for a few years, then moved to Santa Fe to go into business with one of his brothers. "It was a big recreation center," he said, "bowling, ice skating, a cocktail lounge, a real big place, too big after a while." Fifteen years ago, he exercised an option available to all Medal of Honor recipients: he went to work

34

for the VA. He's there now, with the rank of Service Officer, settling claims for veterans and their dependents. Every four years, he goes to Washington with other Medal recipients to attend one of the presidential balls, an invited guest of the incoming administration. On national holidays, he participates with other Medal recipients from New Mexico in local and state ceremonies. But never, until I contacted him, did he agree to talk, on or off the record, with any outsider about his experiences in Korea. Not all Medal of Honor recipients are as shy as Murphy, just as not all are as forthcoming as Ronald Rosser. Many have spoken for the record, modestly and judiciously, as is appropriate for soldiers whose actions have made them public figures. But few have been as reticent for as long as Gerry Murphy, and few have been so forgetful. Ronald Rosser may be an extreme example of recall and storytelling reconstruction; crisis amnesia, when the mind switches to "automatic" in circumstances of fight or flight, is certainly not uncommon, but Gerry Murphy's forty years of silence, forgetfulness, and avoidance is curious. If his heroism is to be understood, so must his silence. The motives for one are hidden in the motives of the other. The origins of both can be found in the life he lived long before he was old enough to enlist in the Marines.

Murphy grew up as the baby in his family. When he was born, his oldest brother was eighteen; the next oldest, sixteen; there was one fourteen, and another was eight. Born to devout Irish Catholics, Gerry was an accident, a gift of the rhythm method. As a child, he was sickly, coddled, and carefully watched by his mother; as a boy, he was sheltered and tutored by brothers old enough to be uncles. His parents had been married by the Benedictine abbot of Pueblo, Colorado; his father, in his youth, had been educated by monks of that abbot's monastery; as soon as Gerry was old enough, he was sent to parochial schools and there he remained for twelve years. His mother understood faith to be obe- 35 dience, and Gerry tried not to disappoint her: he did what she said; he obeyed the nuns; he obeyed the priests; he obeyed and he obeyed. If he broke a rule he was punished, and if he was punished, he understood he was guilty. Every day, Gerry's mother went to mass, and every day, from the time he was ten until he graduated from high school, Gerry served as an altar boy. Even in his first two years of college, when he came home on vacation Gerry helped the priest celebrate mass. It would be an exaggeration to say that Gerry went from being an altar boy to being a Marine, but only because he played baseball all day in the summers of his last two years in college.

Until Gerry was twelve his father was more absent than present, but it was an absence caused by virtue, not vice. His father was known as "the Old Maestro." It was a name that paid tribute to his mastery of the world, its men and machines and the earth they moved. Gerry's father was a civil engineer without a degree; employed by railroads and contractors, he built bridges and roads all across Colorado and New Mexico, western Kansas and Texas, and he did it by dead reckoning and native intelligence, with no formal education past the time he spent with the Benedictines when he was a teenager. The Old Maestro's father had been a sick man who'd died young, leaving Thomas Michael, at age fifteen, head of a household of twelve children and a widow. Thomas Michael didn't turn into the Old Maestro overnight, but at some moment on some job in the middle of some West Texas nowhere, everyone around him, the whole crew from the road bosses to ditch diggers, realized he had "the touch," and the Old Maestro he became. The Old Maestro never went into business on his own, so he never made as much money as he was worth, but he always had a job and he always had the respect of his men. "What do I need money for?" he used to say. "The only reason to have it is to give it away to people who really need it."

Gerry was born in January 1930, and in his first years his mother, his brothers, and nuns guided his life. But in 1942, the Old Maestro returned to Pueblo to become superintendent of the county roads. The Old Maestro came home to stay, and his son never left his side. Gerry sat next to him as he inspected the roads he'd built along the Arkansas River, sat next to him as the Italian vegetable farmers came out and doffed their hats to the Padrone who'd laid the asphalt to carry their produce to market, sat next to him as he drove into the equipment yards, past the rows of trucks and graders and diesel shovels, past the gangs of men who turned and called and waved their respects when they saw him, the Old Maestro with his son, the boss with his boy, the Seignior with his offspring. In 1944, the leaders of the county asked Thomas Michael to become the sheriff. They gave him a desk and a pistol. The Old Maestro put the gun in a drawer and took office. Within a week, the Mafia laid an envelope on his desk. He handed it back, and on Christmas Day 1944, he shut down the Owl's Den and the Silver Moon, the two biggest gambling joints in the county. Four years later, all the Italian vegetable farmers voted him out of office. It was nothing personal: when he died they all came to his funeral, but until then, they sent him back to building roads. Meanwhile, Gerry daydreamed. In his dreams, he imagined himself a rich man, so rich that he created a vast charity to give his money away. "It was going to be named after my father," he said. "I was going to call it The Old Maestro."

The only other thing Gerry dreamed about was baseball. The sickly child had become an athlete. Football in the fall; basketball in the winter; and, summer after summer, baseball as a catcher. The Old Maestro had been one. The youngest of Gerry's brothers had been so good he'd been scouted by the Dodgers. During the war years, in the summers, Gerry worked in the Pueblo steel mills to earn money and keep in shape, but every   37 hour he wasn't tending an open hearth, he was out on a diamond. He went to college on an athletic scholarship, majored in phys. ed., hoped to be a coach. That's what his plans were when the Marines came to his campus and offered a commission to every senior who'd enlist. Marine recruiters were making that same offer in colleges all over the country. When Gerry arrived at boot camp he discovered he'd be sharing a tent with a catcher from Brown, a guard from Princeton, and a back from Iowa State. The Chinese had come south and nearly trapped the 1st Marine Division at the Chosin reservoir; the Marines needed a thousand fresh second lieutenants and they needed them fast: what better place to find them than college athletic departments. Gerry had no objections: one of his brothers had helped build the China–Burma Road; another had crossed the Rhine with Patton. His father had led crews of men and been a sheriff. Gerry's mother had raised him to obey superiors, respect authority, and believe what he was told. He was a healthy mind in a healthy body, ready to do his duty.

Gerry's drill instructor was a racist, anti-Semitic sociopath who was later convicted of killing a black enlisted man with a truck. The first thing the man did was tell the six Jews in Gerry's company that he would never let them survive boot camp because they weren't fit to be Marines. He eventually managed to put four of them in the hospital. Everyone else, Gentile and Jew, football player and track star, lived in fear of him. The parade ground at Parris Island was the biggest man-made open space Gerry had ever seen, but his drill instructor had a voice so Olympian that he could stand at one end and make himself heard at the other. When Gerry couldn't qualify on the rifle range, the DI hung toilet paper from him and made him march at the rear of the formation. Gerry was so terrified of him that, after two weeks of failure, on the last day left to qualify, he scored one level below Expert. Shame, fear, and obedience made him a Marine.

From Parris Island, he was sent to Quantico, where he learned and rehearsed small-unit infantry tactics— tactics well suited for a war of movement but useless for the trench war Korea had become. From Quantico, Gerry was ordered to Pendleton, where he and all the other new officers were given platoons of fresh young enlisted men to order about. This they did, leading them from map coordinate to map coordinate, charging here and there, bonding themselves to their men, preparing to be sent, as units, into the conflict. Instead, in June 1952, Gerry and ninety-nine other second lieutenants were taken from their platoons, marched onto Constellations, and flown to Hawaii, then to Johnson Island, then to Guam, then to Japan, then to Seoul, where they were unloaded on the edge of a city turned to kindling and told to wait for assignments. Gerry's delivered him, one night, to a command bunker near the 38th Parallel, where a second lieutenant spent the night shouting over the radio, rallying his men against a human-wave attack. In the morning, when it was over, the officer packed his gear. "It's all yours, buddy," he said, and left.

The daily routine was the same in Gerry's war as it had been in Rosser's: men fought at night and slept during the day. Rosser, as an enlisted man, could have rested but chose not to. Gerry, as an officer, could also have rested, but chose to set an example: instead of sleeping, he rousted his sergeants, and together with them and his men, each day he rebuilt and strengthened what had been weakened during the night. Such exemplary conduct alone may have caused Manes, the sergeant who later survived the assault on Ungok Hill, to transfer from Gerry's platoon, but Gerry was even more eager: at night, on patrol, instead of staying with his radio operator and runners at the center of his unit, 39

Gerry insisted on walking point. "Walking point?" I
said. "That's not just against regulations. That's a good
way to get killed. Why'd you do it?" Murphy barely
stirred. "Oh—I don't know," he said. "I guess I felt more
confident we'd get where we were going. I had the best
sense of direction in the dark. Night changes things. I
was just better at night than anyone else. I didn't take
the lead 'cause I wanted to get shot. Just the opposite:
I wanted to avoid trouble." One night in November,
though, Gerry couldn't avoid it. He led a squad of twenty
men against a five-man Chinese outpost. Their orders
were to capture prisoners for interrogation. Just as they
were about to surprise the Chinese, Gerry's medical
corpsman panicked and, for some reason, threw an il-
lumination grenade. The Chinese opened fire and Gerry's men fired back. "We had to kill them all," Gerry
said. "Do you remember any of that?" I asked. "Oh
yes," he answered, but said no more. The firing alerted
other Chinese, who pursued them in force. Several of
Gerry's men were wounded. Just barely, he managed
to lead his squad back to safety. It was for this that
Blanchard, the Mustang, recommended Gerry for the
Silver Star. In December, after six months of little food
and no sleep, Gerry went to Japan for R and R. By the
time he returned, Blanchard had volunteered the company to attack Ungok Hill. The rest of the story you
already know.

As Murphy told me about the attack, I stopped him
now and then, trying to learn what he understood about
his own motives. Sometimes I asked him directly, sometimes I pleaded inattention, sometimes I pretended ignorance, always hoping that, by having to repeat or
explain himself, he might add something to what he'd
already said. After four or five hours of listening to his
narrative, its flatness and emptiness, its lack of detail
and self-reflection, I began to think that Murphy was
simply one of those people who don't like to talk or even
think about themselves. He wasn't a rock or a brute or

a fool—he was just unreflective. That's what I thought until, at my urging, he told me again about saying "No" to Captain Blanchard. "What do you think would have happened if you hadn't said 'No'?" I asked. Murphy gave me a blank stare. "What do you mean?" he asked. "Do you think you would have lived?" I asked him. "You said 'No' and some other men went in your place and they died, didn't they?" "Yes," he said. "So," I went on, "your saying 'No' was an act of self-preservation, wasn't it?" Murphy looked genuinely surprised. "Gee," he said, "I never thought of that until you mentioned it. I mean, I never thought what would have happened if I hadn't said 'No.'"

That's when I began to wonder if Murphy's ignorance about himself and his motives wasn't more willful than I'd thought. He'd already told me that attacking Ungok Hill in broad daylight was suicidal. He'd also told me that he was so scared the night before that he'd stayed awake and said his rosary. Hearing all this, I'd concluded that Murphy's refusal to volunteer was a simple act of self-preservation. But Murphy claimed never to have thought about the consequences of his having said "No." He said he hadn't thought about such things for thirty-five years. Such "not thinking" seemed to me equivalent to a man pretending something wasn't there by turning his head away. I began to suspect that Murphy was hiding something.

Of course, all this is speculation. But consider: all his life, by his own account, Murphy had been taught by lesson and example, by his parents, priests, and nuns, to say "Yes" when it was proper and "No" when it wasn't, to respect his elders and defer to their judgment. Murphy had been an obedient child, an obedient boy, and an obedient young man. In all the stories he told me about his youth he never spoke of saying "No." He was a good boy—in fact, an altar boy—who became a good Marine. Whatever habits of obedience he'd learned before boot camp were reinforced by his drill instructor, who used fear and shame to shape his men. Sent to Korea, Murphy became an eager and exemplary young officer. He worked with his men shoulder to shoulder during the day. At night, he led them through darkness. He was a strong, resourceful, and brave young officer whose captain—a self-made man who recognized hard work and courage when he saw it—had already recommended him for the Silver Star, the highest decoration short of the Medal itself. Then, one day, that captain asked Murphy to volunteer to die, and Murphy said "No."

Murphy said "No" for the first time in his life. For twenty-two years, he'd marched in cadence. For the first time, he broke stride. He did it to save his own life. In Korea, he'd come into his own. Taking point was the best example: he'd become a leader instead of a follower. Saying "No" to Blanchard was the sanest kind of refusal. But it was completely uncharacteristic. It was the right thing to do, but it must have felt as wrong as it felt right. A man who'd obeyed authority since he was a child must have had his doubts. Doubts mixed with fear: saying "No" didn't get him completely off the hook. Until the moment of the attack, Murphy feared for his life. He must have been scared at other times, but he never mentioned them in his narrative. In speaking about Ungok Hill, though, Murphy was very plain: he'd been scared to death.

At the moment of the attack, these were his emotions: self-confidence (he'd said "No"), self-doubt (he'd said "No"), and fear. As the attack proceeded, Murphy watched other men die. No matter that he claimed never to have considered the consequences of his refusal; no matter that he said he didn't even remember the names of the men he later rescued, the fact is that, as Murphy watched, what he saw were other men dying in his place. Such deaths must have made him feel guilty. That guilt, combined with whatever self-reproach he may have felt for refusing his captain—all that impelled him not just to do his duty but to do penance. Murphy had been born and bred inside a system that balanced sin with repentance. This is only conjecture, but I think Murphy understood his refusal and its consequences to constitute a sin. A secular explanation for his actions might use the word "compensation": first, he'd refused to obey authority, so, to compensate, to prove his obedience, he not only did his duty but went beyond it; second, he'd shirked his responsibilities and others had died in his place; to compensate for feeling like a coward, he acted more aggressively than he ever had before. Such secular explanations are adequate, but they ignore the life Murphy had lived as a Catholic. As such, his acts of rescue were acts of contrition. His final act of retrieving the bodies of the dead was undertaken in obedience to a warrior code older than the Church. By offering himself and suffering the consequences, Murphy sought absolution.

In the end, he was honored. His citation spoke of "resolute and inspiring leadership, exceptional fortitude and great personal valor." In the end, though, he may not have forgiven himself. The result was thirty-five years of silence and forgetfulness. At its center was his own sense of having sinned. The same guilt that nearly silenced him made Ronald Rosser ring like a bell. Loud or soft, profane or prudish, talkative or quiet, in the end both men acted to atone. Penance brought them honor.

Common Men

JUST AS there's a bureau in the Vatican that reviews the claims of would-be saints, and in the Pentagon there's some office that examines deeds "above and beyond the call," so, in Pittsburgh, there's an office that investigates ordinary people who are said to have risked their lives to save others. The office in Pittsburgh is called the Hero Fund; it was established in 1904 by Andrew Carnegie, the billionaire, who spent the last twenty years of his life giving away his money. The Fund subscribes to a clipping service that sends it news reports of rescues, thousands of them, every year, from all across the United States and Canada. The Fund's staff sorts through the clippings, using a few simple but stringent criteria: the rescuers have to have been civilians, the people they rescued had to have been strangers, and everyone involved, rescuer and rescued alike, had to have been in danger of dying. Over and over again, the Fund questions witnesses and participants, and as it keeps repeating its questions, fewer and fewer rescues meet its standards, so that, in a year in which, for instance, the Fund investigates 3,000 reports of rescue, it bestows medals on only 100 people. The Fund releases

44

the names of these people to the Associated Press, which spreads the news of their good deeds far and wide. At the end of every year, the Fund itself publishes a pamphlet that briefly describes each rescuer and rescued in prose as laconic as a police report.

Since the Fund believes that publicity given to good deeds benefits everyone, a copy of its most recent annual report was mine for the asking. Most of the deeds described in it were rescues of people in danger of drowning or of being burned to death. Now and then, there were descriptions of people saved from being raped, beaten, or murdered. I decided to inquire into rescues from such assaults for two reasons, one more personal than the other. The objective reason requires little explanation: in this part of the century, nature has done less harm to us than we've done to ourselves. The assault of one person on another is like a war. Any intervention that stops such harm contains all the possibilities of peace. I thought if I could understand a small kind of goodness, I might understand a larger one. There was something else, though, that I wanted to understand: when I was a boy, I'd once wandered into the wrong place and been trapped and beaten. I was fourteen, working my first summer job. My boss sent me on an errand into a bad neighborhood, but he didn't tell me about the neighborhood. I walked down a street lined with big, dilapidated houses. Men and women sat on their porches and stared at me. A gang of boys came up behind me and pushed me into an alley. I looked back over my shoulder: the people on the porches were still staring at me. The boys surrounded me; they began to beat me. I fell down. As I looked up, two men broke into the circle and saved me. According to the Hero Fund, the men wouldn't have qualified as heroes, but I remember what it felt like to be rescued from other people. I felt grateful, but, also, I was baffled: I didn't know why I'd been beaten, or why the people on the porches hadn't helped me, or why—if they hadn't—the 45 two men had. Maybe the boys attacked me for the same reason the people who watched did nothing: maybe the kind of person I was, alone in the kind of place I was in, deserved to be attacked, like a rabbit who'd blundered into wolves. If that was so, then why had the men stopped the boys from hurting me more than they had? Intervention and indifference: the men saved me while other people turned aside. I didn't understand it then, and I don't now. For all these reasons, large and small, I decided to inquire why some people stopped others from being killed.

The description of each rescue in the annual report the Fund sent me gave the name of the rescuer as well as his or her age and profession. I read of a short-order cook who'd foiled an armed kidnapper, a waitress who'd saved a policeman from being shot with his own gun, a housepainter who'd rescued a little girl from a lunatic armed with a knife. There were descriptions of the deeds of a real estate salesman, a telephone technician, a carpenter, a college student, a stockbroker, a secretary, even someone having the job of "rubber and plastics fabricator." What stopped me, though, were descriptions of two rescues from armed assault in which the heroes were described as "writers." I had heard of writers who'd become presidents and prime ministers; I knew of writers who'd become thieves; I even knew of writers who wrote, but I'd never heard of writers who'd rescued people from death. Sitting staring at a blank page, hour after hour, is risky, but I'd never heard of anyone dying from it. The two writers interested me, not just because they were like me, but because they weren't: the boy I once was, the boy who'd been trapped, beaten, and then rescued, that boy had become a writer, but the writer had never repaid the boy's debt. I may have written some books in my life, but books were nothing but messages in bottles. I'd tossed more than one over the side, but I'd never taken the dive myself.

According to the Hero Fund, though, there were two writers in this world who had. As I read and reread the brief descriptions of the men and what they did, I was intrigued by the similarities between them: both had rescued people from men armed with knives, both had nearly died of stab wounds, and both had the same first name. Tim Mosher had stopped a man from slashing and raping a woman trapped in her apartment. Tim Chorcoran had gone up against four men who would have stabbed to death a passerby if Chorcoran hadn't intervened. What they'd done was brave, but it was their names that made me wonder: "Tim" was some crippled little boy in Dickens, not some gallant man on a white horse. "Brave men with frail names," I thought. "That might be something to talk about."

I soon discovered I was wrong: the investigators at the Hero Fund had paid more attention to the men's deeds than to their jobs. Neither of the two Tims was a writer. They both wanted to be, but they weren't. The closest Chorcoran came to writing was tapping at a word processor, transcribing the Bible for a millionaire. That whole story, in all its loony piety, comes later. As to Mosher, he only wrote if he had absolutely nothing better to do. Or, as he said, "I never did make much progress, 'cause I'd always be thinking, 'Shit, I could be out doing something. I could be out making money, not just sitting there.'"

Mosher's way of making money was driving a cab in New York City; he'd been doing it for five years the night he saved the woman. His ambition was to make movies. The night of the rescue, he hadn't been doing either. The man who owned the cab Mosher leased had just fired him, and he hadn't worked for so long on a film crew, he'd begun to believe he never would again. The night he became a hero, he was sitting alone stranded in his apartment with nothing to do but work on a screenplay he'd been nursing along, a little some-   47 thing called "Vampire Taxi" about a cabbie who took more than money from his passengers.

I

Mosher told me his story in bits and pieces, scattered across half a morning, an afternoon, and an evening. When I met him, nearly a year after he'd rescued the woman, he wasn't driving a cab or pecking away at a screenplay or even living alone anymore—in fact, he'd just returned to his fiancée's apartment after three days as a production assistant for a film crew shooting a car ad. A white Saab was supposed to have raced along the seashore, turned into a sea gull, and then soared off into the sunset. Nothing had gone right, not the light or the car or the birds, and Mosher, whose job was to make sure everyone had what they needed to do their jobs, had spent all his time racing around trying to locate enough mineral water and yogurt to keep everyone happy. Groggy from managing too many details with too little sleep, Mosher had trouble at first keeping track of his own story. Even after a couple of cups of coffee, he'd slip into a mumble, then stop and apologize. Half his family—his father's side—he said, talked like that: old-time upstate New Yorkers, they preferred one-word answers, yeses and noes; anything else they muttered. As the morning went on, Mosher mumbled less; whole sentences flashed out, crisp and quick. After something close to an aria, I asked about it. "You more awake?" I said. He shook his head. He knew how he sounded. "It's my mom," he said. Her side of the family were Italians, sharp-tongued and volatile. Listening to the upstate New Yorkers collide with the Italians in Mosher's speech was like watching a cold front mix with warm air. Since Mosher had come of age in the sixties, he also used the argot of that period, a word like "crash" to mean "fall asleep exhausted," or "scope out" to mean 48 "investigate." All these expressions he strung together

with more than a few "you know's." He was a storyteller who had to be prompted, not because he was
reticent, but because he was disorganized, so disorganized that—not out of malice—he even forgot one of
his own brothers. Part of the time, we sat at a table,
twenty stories above the street, him losing track, me
asking him to repeat himself; the rest of the time, we
sat outside, on a bench across from the Guggenheim,
watching cabs fight their way downtown, while he
meandered and I tried not to forget the order of his life.
To tell his story as he told it would be exasperating, but
it did have its moments. One of them was the night of
the rescue:

Mosher sat until 1:00 a.m. fretting over his screenplay. He'd type four lines, shuffle his notes, stand up,
stretch, look out the window, turn on the radio, go to
the bathroom, come back and pop a beer. He'd type
four more lines, check his notes, make a phone call,
finish his beer, stand up, stretch, and start again. That
went on until he decided he'd suffered enough. It was
time to take a walk and call it a night.

He was getting ready to go out the door when he
heard his upstairs neighbor moving furniture. It was a
little late for that, he thought, but he knew she kept odd
hours. That's nearly all he knew about her. He'd met
her on the stairs. He thought maybe she worked for the
hospital that owned the building. Maybe a nurse, but
he didn't know. An upstairs New York neighbor, live
and let live. He checked his keys, then he heard a
thump, like a fall, then he heard a scream. He'd never
heard that before. He went upstairs. "But why?" I asked.
"I thought about that," he said, "when I was in the
hospital. All I can tell you is that if I hadn't gone up
and something bad had happened to her, I didn't think
I could've lived with myself." That's what he thought
later. At the moment he heard the scream, he didn't
consult his conscience. He was a man who'd driven a
cab for five years, a man who'd seen plenty of nasty 49

situations begin and end in his back seat with no one getting hurt and him even getting a tip. Mosher was no martial arts expert, but he trusted his own wits and he didn't expect the worst when he went upstairs.

The door to the woman's apartment was ajar. He pushed it open with his foot. He didn't know it then, but he'd made his last voluntary choice of the night. The door swung into a narrow hallway. Two people stepped out of the side bedroom. One was Mosher's neighbor; one was the building's janitor. The janitor had talked his way in by saying he'd come to fix a leak. The only tool he'd brought, though, was an eight-inch kitchen knife. He'd taken Mosher's neighbor into her bedroom and laid her on the bed. He'd just slashed her throat and was about to rape her when he heard the door open. Now he stood behind the woman with his arm around her waist. The woman's face was covered with blood. The janitor's face was calm. The hallway was quiet and dark. "What are you doing, man?" Mosher asked. The janitor didn't answer. He acted as if he hadn't heard the question because Mosher wasn't there. Mosher spoke the woman's name. The janitor looked away. The woman opened her eyes as wide as she could. The janitor nudged her down the hallway; the woman tried to pull away. "What the hell are you doing, man?" Mosher asked. The janitor walked her deeper into the apartment. "Get away from her," Mosher said. The woman twisted against the janitor's arm. "What are you doing, you motherfucker? Let her go." The woman pulled loose and rushed past Mosher out the door, onto the landing. Mosher and the janitor were alone in the hallway. The janitor was a little man, but well muscled and strong. Mosher was long-limbed and wiry. He knew he outreached the man, but he also knew the janitor had something in his hand. The janitor raised his hand; Mosher saw the knife. The janitor brought it down into Mosher's chest.

50   What he'd done was slice open Mosher's mammary

artery, a branch of a branch of the superior vena cava, a major blood vessel. Mosher didn't know it, but he'd begun to bleed to death. He stumbled backwards. "I must've fallen off the knife," he said. He didn't feel hurt. "I was stunned. I thought, 'Oh shit. What have I got myself into?'" He pivoted and lurched out the door, onto the landing. His neighbor was there, pounding on all the other doors. "Open up. Open up," she screamed. No one did. Mosher grabbed her and pulled her after him down the stairs, into his apartment. "All I was thinking was to get away from that son of a bitch," he said. He locked the door behind them. His neighbor apologized. "I'm bleeding all over your apartment," she said. Mosher handed her a towel to hold around her throat. He looked down at himself. His shirt was red but he felt all right. Well enough to call 911. The operator asked him his address, then his phone number, then his name. By the time the operator asked him what happened, Mosher had lost track of the conversation. He heard something splashing and looked down. He was wearing cowboy boots. His boots were in a puddle of blood. He moved his foot. His boot was full of blood. There was blood running down under his shirt, a stream of it, running down his pants, into his boot, then overflowing onto the floor. His blood. He heard the operator asking him for details again. "I don't know, man," he said. "All I can tell you is she's cut and I'm cut. And I'm going down. I sure as hell hope you get here before we both do."

He lay down on the couch, on his belly. His body felt heavy. Too heavy for him to make it do what he wanted. His mind was clear. He didn't want to lie down on his back because he didn't want to aspirate blood. He sank deeper in the couch. "What a shitty place to die," he thought. His mind flickered. He could barely hear the cops pounding on the door. "Police. Police. Open up. Open up," they shouted, but his neighbor wouldn't unlock the door. "How do I know who you are?" she screamed. She was sure it was the janitor come back to kill them. The cops put their radios against the door. "Listen," they yelled. "Here's our radios. We're police. Unlock the goddamn door." She let them in.

Mosher opened his eyes and saw two emergency medical technicians standing over him. "Do you mind if we cut open your shirt?" one asked. Very polite. "Shit, man," said Mosher. "No problem. I don't mind at all." They carried him down the stairs and slid him into the ambulance. His mind was clear again. They were taking him to New York Hospital. He knew that. He'd driven the route so many times, he knew every hump and bump on the way. "Good," he thought. "Hurry." They tried to open his mouth to push an airway down his throat. He wanted to help them, but he couldn't make his mouth open. He tried, but he couldn't unlock his jaws. He felt the blood sloshing around in his chest. "Hurry," he thought, "hurry, I'm dying." He wanted to say it, but he couldn't move his lips.

They wheeled him into the hospital. "I saw where I was, but if I would've known what they were going to do, I might've got up and left." What they were going to do was "crash" him; they were going to open his chest, but they weren't going to use anesthesia. His blood pressure was so low, if they put him to sleep he wouldn't wake up. Mosher flickered out as they slid him onto the table. They started some IVs and called the heart surgeon. The surgeon thought they'd have to do a bypass. Mosher woke up just as they were slicing open his chest. He heard the surgeon ask for "spreaders." He heard the spreaders clatter on the tray. They were about to "crack" his chest—crack apart his ribs and go in, looking for the bleeder. He was lucky he didn't know what to expect. "The worst goddamn pain in the whole fuckin' world," he said. He screamed and screamed and then he passed out. The surgeon found the mammary artery, clamped it, and sutured it. They closed him up and gave him blood. Six units on the table, ten more by the time he was finally released, one and a third times his total blood volume.

He was in intensive care for three days, on a respirator, full of morphine. The first time he woke up, he saw red dragons dancing across the ceiling. He smiled. "They must've got their dope from China," he thought, and passed out. The next time he woke up, he thought he was still seeing things. On one side of the bed stood the woman he loved—the woman who was to become his fiancée. A few weeks before the rescue, she'd told him she never wanted to see him again. On the other side of the bed stood his father and mother. They'd written him off years before as a loser. They were all looking at him. The woman had tears in her eyes. His parents were smiling. He wasn't seeing things. The *Post*, the *Daily News*, *Newsday*, and the *Times*—every paper in New York wrote about him. "Hero," they called him. "Samaritan," they called him. "Writer," they said. It was a happy ending, a real classic, as good as any he could have written. Better, in fact, considering what an unhappy life he'd led.

Mosher was a floater who'd been cast adrift when he was ten; for the next twenty-five years, he'd kept trying to drop anchor. His parents had cut their own ties early, crossing class and ethnic lines to marry. Both came from a carpet mill town in the Mohawk Valley, where nationality and religion determined a man's job, and a man's job defined his family's place in a hierarchy that descended from the millionaires' mansions on the top of the hill to the flats on the "wrong side of the river" where the most recent immigrants lived. Every generation, a few people managed to work their way one step up the slope, but no one married back across the river. The Moshers lived halfway up the hill, neither rich nor poor, but with an "Old Yankee" bloodline that made them feel better than most. That was why Mosher's grandparents were appalled when Mosher's father mar-   53 ried Mosher's mother: not only was she Catholic; she was also Italian, the child of a family "fresh off the boat."

The Second War and the U.S. Navy had given Mosher's father his first freedom. He'd returned, trained as a flight engineer, determined not to live and die like his ancestors. Mosher wasn't sure how or where his parents had met, in a bar maybe, but one thing he knew: his mother had broken as many rules as his father. An arranged marriage, yearly pregnancies, mass every Sunday till she died—she'd married a Protestant and escaped. The two moved to Brooklyn, then out to Long Island. Before they and people like them arrived, towns like Hicksville had been quaint hamlets surrounded by potato fields. Soon the fields sprouted houses and the houses obliterated the towns. New streets, new schools, new stores, new people—the suburbs had only one tradition: men worked, women kept house, and the kids went to school.

Mosher was the second-born of four brothers. Not as studious as his oldest brother, not as obedient as the youngest, not as wild as the brother closest to him in age, he was a textbook middle child, too young to be a leader, too old to be a follower, adrift in the birth order. He went to a parochial school until he was ten. He loved the rules, the order, and the certainty. He loved knowing his place. He begged his mother to send him on to Catholic middle school. His mother refused. She hadn't left her family and married a Protestant on a whim. "No son of mine is going to be taught by nuns all his life," she said. She thought she was setting her son free. Mosher felt as if she'd thrown him overboard.

Puberty sank him. Good Catholic boys knew autoeroticism to be a mortal sin, whose forgiveness required prayer and repentance. At public school, Mosher met boys who weren't Catholic and who not only masturbated but boasted about it. Mosher tried it, liked it, and began to doubt his faith. Meanwhile, in typical subur-

ban fashion, his parents' marriage began to come apart.
The tradition of "men go to work and women stay
home" infuriated Mosher's mother, especially because
the work Mosher's father did gave him more opportunity to leave home than he'd had since he'd broken free
from the mill town. Mosher's father had hopped,
skipped, and jumped from naval aviation to Grumman
to Republic to the Civil Aeronautics Board, where he
served as a crash site investigator. That meant he kept
his bag packed, and when a plane crashed, the phone
rang, and he left. What he left were four boys and a
wife who hadn't defied her parents so she could be
trapped in a tract house with four kids. What happened
when Mosher's father returned was as suburban as a
backyard barbecue: Mosher's dad would unpack; Mosher's mom would begin to complain; the two would
start to argue. Nothing would be settled, but next time,
when Mosher's dad left, he knew the welcome he'd get
when he came home, so he found an excuse to stay
away longer. That cycle of louder arguments and longer
absences coincided with Mosher's first year in high
school.

To enter high school in 1966 was to come of age when
sex, drugs, and rock and roll made adolescent rebellion
a full-time job. Mosher smoked marijuana during the
week and took LSD on the weekends. The LSD completed his loss of faith. "I used it like Drano," he said.
"It flushed the Catholicism right out of my brain. That's
how I got to be an ex-Catholic. But being an ex-Catholic's its own kind of religion." Mosher read the Koran,
protested the war in Vietnam, and let his hair grow. He
also developed a severe case of acne. Today, faint scars
runnel his skin, but his long, creased face belongs to a
man who's lived long enough to earn his good looks.
When he was sixteen, though, the acne made him feel
ugly and ashamed. Sometimes he picked fights; most
of the time he avoided people. Once he put his fist
through the window of a door. His parents decided he   55

was their punishment for a bad marriage: a drug addict, a hippie dropout. They used him to blame each other: "If you'd only been a better mother!" led to "If you'd only been a better father!" led to "Your mother and I are headed for a divorce and it's all because of you!"

Mosher took the hint and went looking for another family. What he found was the mother of a friend. The woman seems to have been the sort who took in stray cats and dogs, and damaged kids. Mosher ate at her table, told her his troubles, even had a romance with her daughter. When he graduated from high school, his own parents told him he was on his own. They didn't so much disown him as write him off as a bad risk. College, they said, would be wasted on him; a job was his problem, not theirs. Mosher appealed to his second mother. She took care of retarded people at a state mental hospital. She found Mosher a job there, caring for dead souls. The job was to help clean and feed forty severely retarded men, men who had been so damaged and were so isolated from the world that their attendants could have been zookeepers. One man had been in bed so long that the orderlies—who did nothing but turn him—called him "the Pancake." Another sat all day in the corridor, collapsed like a puppet. Each time a nurse walked past, it was as if someone twitched the strings attached to his head; up it jerked and out of his mouth came "I love you. Talk to me. I love you," over and over again, until the nurse passed. Then the strings went slack and the head sank back until the next nurse and the next twitch, the next jerk and the next refrain. All day, in the noise and stench of a monkey house, Mosher wiped, carried, washed, and fed. He lasted a year and a half.

He lasted that long because he wanted to qualify for free college tuition, offered by the state as an incentive to workers not to quit. Unfortunately, papers like the *Post* and *Newsday* began to print horror stories about hospitals like the one where Mosher worked. The state reacted to the scandal by freezing its mental health budget. That freeze included benefits and left Mosher stranded: he wanted to quit, but if he did, he might fall through the cracks between the old rules and the new ones sure to come. He held on, waiting for the freeze to end. One morning while driving to work, he brooded about his predicament. He had a new car, a Datsun. His father had signed the note since Mosher had a job. He'd have to pay his father back, he knew. One more trap, he thought. It was raining, then the rain changed to hail. A big Oldsmobile was tailgating him. Up ahead, a Cadillac jackknifed. Mosher hit the brakes. He slammed into the Caddy. The Olds slammed into him. The trap closed and smashed him flat. No one was hurt, but the Datsun was totaled. The insurance company paid it off. Mosher took it as a sign: he broke free, quit his job, and headed for Manhattan.

He found work as a clerk in an expensive shop that treated its merchandise better than its employees. Eventually, he found a job selling posters in the museum store of the Met. There, he met a woman from Norway. She said she loved him but needed a green card. They married; she became a citizen, then became pregnant. Outside their apartment on the Lower East Side, junkies ranted and raved, strung out on a combination of booze and methadone. Mosher's wife began to nag him: this was no place to raise a family; Mosher wasn't cut out to be a clerk; they needed more money; they needed more room; he needed to go to college. It was 1974; he was twenty-two years old. He applied to NYU for financial aid. The university offered him tuition for one semester. He quit his job, went to class during the day, found a cab to drive at night. He was too tired to study and too exhausted to drive. He dropped out and went back to being a clerk. His wife wasn't pleased. He counted it as one more failure.

Two years went by. He and his wife still lived in the same place, three rooms, two adults and a child. Outside on the street, Scorsese, the film director, shot *Taxi Driver*. "All those pimps and hookers," said Mosher. "It could've been real. They didn't need to hire actors." Two more years went by. Early one evening he was out walking his dog along the East River. A Puerto Rican kid came toward him, pushing his bike, walking beside the wall that dropped eight feet to the water. The tide was ripping out to sea. The kid walked toward Mosher, leaning over the embankment, talking to the water. Mosher knew him. "What's going on?" he asked as the kid came close. "I'm talking to this guy," the kid said, and nodded at the water. Mosher looked down and saw an old Ukrainian, a man he knew, swimming along, his hat still on his head. The kid said, "Me and my buddy, we saw him. He stood there, then he just jumped in. I been talkin' to him, trying to get him to stay close." The kid kept walking and talking; the old man paddled along, not saying anything. "I sent my buddy to go get the rescue," said the kid. "I'm gonna keep him talkin' till the boat gets here." The old man watched him and kept paddling while the river sucked him out to sea. Mosher looked down at the old man and thought, "No way in hell can I get him out. There's no handholds. I can jump in, but there's nothing to climb out." The only things between the old man and the ocean were the pylons of the Williamsburg Bridge. Mosher and the kid kept talking to the guy, trying to keep him near the wall, hoping the fireboat was on its way. Without a word, the old man turned and breaststroked out, toward the middle of the river. They watched him until he was nothing but a hat. They watched until he was nothing at all. He'd wanted to kill himself and he'd done it. "And there wasn't a fuckin' thing I could do but watch," said Mosher. That watching, he remembered.

In the spring, he reapplied to NYU. The lady who interviewed him was old enough to be his mother. He told her his troubles; she listened and took pity. "I told her I hadn't been the greatest student in high school,"

Mosher said. "But I told her I'd settled down. I was twenty-seven; I had a family; I was serious. I was ready to do something with my life." She asked him what he was interested in. He told her filmmaking, not the art, but the craft. His ancestors had been carpet mill mechanics, not poets. He wanted to learn how to make something, not dream it up. "I must've said something right, 'cause I walked out of there with a full scholarship." In fact, he'd been blessed by his third mother.

He studied hard, but he was as much a loner as he'd been in high school. He didn't have acne anymore and he didn't use drugs, but the other students were nine years younger than he was. He could talk with them about filmmaking, but at the end of the day, when they went out, he went home. After four years, everyone had formed friendships that became networks that led to jobs. Everyone but Mosher. When he knocked on doors, he stood alone. What made it worse was that it was 1982, the bottom of a bad recession. All sorts of experienced people were looking for film work. Someone who'd just graduated from NYU didn't stand a chance. The few part-time jobs Mosher found as a production assistant led nowhere. His wife lost her patience. She didn't complain anymore, she accused: she'd worked while he'd studied; now it was his turn, but he sat idle; he was a failure, nothing but a failure. She took their child and left. Mosher went to bed and didn't get up for two weeks.

When he recovered, he went back to driving a cab. To be exact, he leased one from an owner. He chose to drive at night. "I wanted to keep my options open," he said. Not that there were many, even if his schedule hadn't cut him off from the day world. His job began at 4 p.m. He'd work the rush hour, then the airports. At 10:00, he and his buddies would converge on Sheridan Square to work the gay scene. It was 1983–84 and the baths, bars, and clubs hadn't collapsed yet. There were plenty of good fares, one after the other, until 3

59

a.m. At 5:00 he had to return his cab to the garage. Then he and his buddies would get together, go to a diner, drink a few beers, and go home to bed. At 2:00 in the afternoon, Mosher would wake up and begin again. He worked three days and netted $390. Extra days only dulled him; if he wasn't alert, he made less money. Most people burned out after four years. Mosher lasted five.

He lasted that long because he liked the life. He liked the night and he liked the edge. He liked knowing things secret and obscure: not just Chinese massage parlors and floating Korean blackjack games, but the probable outcome of every fare before they climbed into his cab, the who, what, and where of people before they told him their destinations. That kind of knowing made him money and kept him safe. Sometimes he drove with a knife, but most of the time he used his wits, knowing just how much and how hard to answer an angry drunk or a cokehead who'd turned mean: say too little and they kept pushing; say too much and they felt provoked. He was never robbed, never hurt, and, for a while, he even made a living, but only for a while.

"Driving was always some kind of a gamble," he said, "but after a couple years, it was like the odds started changing." More and more cabbies started getting killed, twenty in Mosher's last year, shot in the back of the head. By 1985, the gay scene had folded and he and his buddies had to find new clients. Mosher settled on Japanese piano bars: Japanese businessmen went in right after work and drank until closing time, when they staggered out, looking for $40 rides home to West-chester. If Mosher was lucky, he'd bag two a night, but he wasn't lucky that often. He started growing tired of the drunks who fell asleep or the ones who threw up or the others who forgot where they wanted to go or didn't even know when they climbed in. After work, his buddies all talked about what they were *really* going to do after they stopped the driving. Mosher kept trying to find film jobs, but the producers he met were worse than the drunks he drove. Worse because at least the drunks were honest. One producer he knew was arrested by the FBI for bank fraud; another, an insurance agent with big ideas, disappeared after he pocketed some premiums. No matter what Mosher tried, he couldn't find film work. He felt trapped. Again.

By New Year's 1987, Mosher was six months behind on his rent. He lived in a ratty building on the edge of East Harlem. A big hospital had bought it to convert or tear it down. Mosher made a deal with the new owners; if they'd forget what he owed he'd leave when they wanted without a fight. The hospital was happy to agree: to get rid of a tenant without hiring a lawyer was worth six months' rent and more. Mosher still had a place to sleep, but the rest of his life was coming apart. He couldn't make a living doing what he wanted, and he couldn't make a living doing what he didn't want. The woman he loved, a woman he'd met just after his wife had left him, had said goodbye. "Get another job," she'd said. "I'm tired of your upside-down days." Mosher had gone out with other people, but all he could talk about was the woman who wasn't there. The only chance he had to change things was a book he'd thought up with another driver: every cabbie in New York used a driver's guide for routes, out-of-town rates, and street addresses. The one everyone used was out of date. Mosher and his buddy planned a new one. They'd even found a publisher and made an appointment to see him. His offices were out on Long Island. They planned to drive there in Mosher's cab.

The morning of their appointment, the cab wouldn't start. They popped the hood: the alternator was dead. The cab belonged to a man who owned five of them. Mosher called the man's office: no answer. He called the man's beeper: no response. He called the man's home and left a message on his machine. Mosher and his buddy had three hours until their appointment.

Every half hour, Mosher called the man's numbers, stacking messages on his answering machine. The time of their appointment came and went. Mosher's buddy left. Mosher kept calling. At four o'clock in the afternoon, the man returned Mosher's calls. "What the fuck you want, calling me at home?" he said. Mosher told him. "Why'd you wait till now to lay this shit on me?" the man said. Mosher told him he'd been trying to reach him all day. "The hell you have," said the man. Mosher laughed. "What is this?" he said. "Are you calling me a liar?" "You figure it out, smart-ass," said the man, "and when you do, try this: you're fired. Got it? Fired. Now fuck off." It was five o'clock in the afternoon. Mosher had a dead cab, no job, no book contract, no film work, no girlfriend, and all night to sit and think about it.

That was the prelude, then, to what he did. Fresh anger, restlessness, and resentment fueled his climb up the stairs. Experience as a cabdriver gave him the confidence to push open his neighbor's door. Years of failure, drift, and frustration had preceded all this. He was not only empty-handed at the moment he went up the stairs; he'd been empty-handed since he was a boy. He'd been an outcast in his family and an outcast in high school. His first job had been to care for men who were as good as dead; his last job had exiled him from the waking world. In between, he'd worked as a clerk and failed as a husband and provider. He'd gone to school to learn a trade he couldn't practice. He'd stood by and watched a man drown. His life had been a series of traps and bafflements, interspersed with appeals to women old enough to be his mother.

A conventional way to explain what Mosher did is to say he had nothing left to lose. But consider the emotional logic of that: would you, if you were starving, give a hungry man your food? Mosher still had his life and his hope to lose. Those were his treasures. His garbage has already been described. The question, though, is:

what did Mosher have to gain? Some might say that
Mosher overcame his failure and frustration to do what
he did. In fact, failure and frustration were the cause
of his actions; they enabled him to act; they compelled
him to act. If he hadn't been so unhappy, if he hadn't
felt so trapped, he wouldn't have acted. Because he
needed to be saved, he saved someone else. Because he
was trapped, he freed another.

II

The newspapers declared Mosher a hero because he fit
the part: he was the right sex and race; he had the looks;
he even had the right kind of job. Add that to rescuing
a damsel in distress, set it underneath inch-high headlines, and out came a news story everyone recognized.
Timothy Chorcoran didn't add up like that.

First, there was his appearance: his face looked as if
it was on loan from a children's television program. He
had big front teeth like Goofy; he had a huge, hinged
jaw like Howdy Doody; his eyes were as big and blue
as Pinocchio's. He was no midget, but at five feet eight
inches he didn't look big enough to have taken on four
men with knives. Besides that, there was his voice: it
was a nice voice, a mild and mellow voice, a little
cracked, but good enough for singing "When You Wish
Upon a Star." Which is what I expected him to do when
I met him. He was so earnest and so well-meaning but
so easily amazed he might have been twelve instead of
twenty-eight. He wasn't stupid, though. He knew he
gave the impression of being simpleminded, so he made
sure I understood. When he was twelve, he said, he'd
been tested in grade school: the nuns decided he was
gifted. He may have been bright, but he still acted as if
he hadn't grown up: driving around with me in his old
Chevy, he stopped to buy some gas. A fill-up entitled
him to a free car wash. His Chevy was so pocked and
faded and crusted with rust that no amount of soap and   63

water could have made it look better. I asked him about that, but he just smiled and shook his head. "I know," he said, "but I love watching the suds." We drove into the shed behind the station and the machine started. "Wow!" he said as soapy strips of cloth swayed across the windshield. "They look just like tentacles!" A big circular brush whirled down upon us and Chorcoran laughed and flinched as if he were afraid. "That was great!" he said as we drove out the other side. "Let's do it again!" And so we did. Later in the day, we went out to dinner. A tossed salad came with the meal. As the waitress put the bowls of lettuce and tomatoes in front of us, Chorcoran took his from her hand and drew it close to his face. "Look at those tomatoes," he said. "Where do you ever get stuff like this? It's the middle of the winter." He looked at the pale, pink tomatoes as if they were guavas or passion fruits. The waitress looked at me as if to ask, "Is he kidding?" I raised my eyebrows. "I think they grow 'em down in Mexico some-where," she said. Chorcoran cocked his head like a dog listening to music. "Mexico?" he said. "All the way from Mexico? That's just amazing!" The waitress looked at me again. I kept a straight face. She shrugged and walked away.

After dessert, Chorcoran told me what he did for a living. He said he killed mosquitoes. "You do what?" I said. "I used to," he said. "I used to kill mosquitoes. I did it for seven years. Then I quit." "How come?" I asked. "So I could be a better Christian." When Tim Mosher had told me about Scorsese making *Taxi Driver* on the street outside his apartment, I'd thought, "Sure. Perfect. The taxi driver and *Taxi Driver*. It's almost too good to be true." But when Chorcoran told me about the mosquitoes, all I could think of was a fairy tale, the one about the little tailor who killed flies. He'd killed seven, then boasted. "Seven," he said, loud enough for everyone to hear. "Seven with a single blow!" A mean and terrible giant heard him. "Seven men!" thought the

64

giant, and ran away. Chorcoran had never killed anyone, and he'd never bragged about it, but he seemed
the most unlikely of heroes—too short, too silly-looking,
too boyish, and too naïve. "Instead of fighting four
guys," I thought, "he should have been home in paja-
mas watching cartoons."

Instead—as Chorcoran told it—he'd been home reading the Bible. Once he'd stopped killing mosquitoes, he
said, he'd read it every night. He'd also gone to work,
full-time, for an old man named Mr. Liberty. "He had
me transcribe the Bible," Chorcoran said. I tried not to
laugh, but a smile leaked out. Chorcoran saw it and
grinned. My amusement pleased him. Later, I learned
that in grade school, to make up for his small size, he'd
been the class clown. "Better they laugh with you than
at you" might have been his motto. My smile made
Chorcoran happy. It consoled him. He treated me like
a guest: better I should be amused than bored. He knew
Mr. Liberty made a good story, so, once the waitress
cleared the table, Chorcoran told me about him and,
once he finished with Mr. Liberty, he told me more
about himself.

In his long life, Chorcoran said, Mr. Liberty had made
and lost several fortunes, all in the oil business. His last
million he decided to spend on something worthy, and
what could be more worthy than a computer concordance of the Scriptures? As long as the money held out,
he paid Chorcoran to sit, day after day, in front of a PC
and cross-index the Bible, already transcribed on floppy
disks. Chorcoran did this in the back room of what had
once been a Gulf station, a few blocks from his little
house in an old Irish neighborhood in Cleveland. Long
ago, the neighborhood's brick churches had been nailed
shut, its banks had turned into funeral homes, its family
mansions into rooming houses, its gas stations into li-
quor stores. Mr. Liberty had converted the Gulf station
into offices by hanging out a sign that read "Liberty
Refining/Garden of Gethsemane Publishing." It was   65

the sign that had brought Chorcoran wandering in one Saturday afternoon years before. He'd worked for Mr. Liberty, on and off, part-time, all the years he'd killed mosquitoes. Every time he and Mr. Liberty's other employees reached the end of whatever project Mr. Liberty had devised, the old man would set a new goal, and each time they achieved that, Mr. Liberty would set another, so that his concordance grew and grew, like a backyard cathedral, its towers made of nothing but bits and bytes and floppy disks, rising higher and higher until there was only enough money left to pay one full-time employee, and that employee was Timothy Chorcoran. For seven months, Chorcoran had typed and retyped the Bible during the day and studied it at night.

The night he did his deed, said Chorcoran, he was reading St. Matthew. Months before, he'd enrolled in a Bible study correspondence course, and had made his way through the Sermon on the Mount, until he reached a choice passage about hypocrites. That night, he sat alone in his upstairs front room, at a table by an open window, reading about Scribes and Pharisees: "For they bind heavy burdens, grievous to be borne. . . . And love the uppermost rooms. . . . And the chief seats and greetings in the markets." Outside, Chorcoran heard a noise; outside there was always noise; his house faced a main street, four lanes of traffic on its way to the suburbs. Even late at night there were calls and shouts and radios, people on the street, sick of their rooms. That night, though, Chorcoran said he heard something different.

"It sounded like lions," he said. He looked out his windows. Across the street was a funeral home parking lot. He saw a man, then a group of men chasing him. Chorcoran jumped up and ran downstairs, out onto his porch. A minute before, he'd been reading, "Woe unto you, hypocrites!"; now he was looking for his baseball bat. He spun around: no bat. He leaped the steps, lowered his head, and charged across the street. As I listened, I could see Chorcoran: Tiny Tim turned into the Incredible Hulk. "Don't get me mad. Don't get me mad," the Hulk used to say. Then it would happen, something he couldn't control: his muscles would swell, his shirt split, and naked to the waist, engorged with rage, his fists like iron hammers, the Hulk would descend upon his foes.

That night, the Hulk's foes were four drunk Mexicans. Chorcoran ran straight at them, bellowing like a bull. He didn't know who they were, any more than they knew who they were knifing. They'd been driving around all night, drinking beer and arguing. A car had cut them off; they'd chased it, lost it, gotten out, and gone looking. The man they found was walking home to bed. He'd done nothing to offend them, except he was a white man in the wrong place at the wrong time. They'd stuck nine holes in him by the time Chorcoran scattered them. Two went one way; two went the other. One kept running, but the other three looked over their shoulders and stopped when they saw the Incredible Hulk was nothing but a little white guy, even smaller than the one they'd been sticking. They circled back, two to the left, one to the right. Chorcoran knew he was in trouble and started backpedaling, but they caught him. The one in front kicked him in the belly; the two behind stabbed him in the back. He fell, pulled himself up, turned tail, and ran. He'd distracted them long enough to save the victim's life; he didn't know that then; all he was thinking about was saving his own. Without looking, he ran across the street back to his house. Months later, that's what he dreamed about, the not looking. "That's what scared me," he said. "I could have been hit by a car. It's a miracle I made it."

The noise of the fight, the bellows and shouts, woke the neighbors. Lights went on; shades went up; people stepped out onto their porches. No one saw Chorcoran. He was inside by then, holding his back, peeping out the window. The police came, an ambulance arrived; 67

the victim was evacuated. Chorcoran held a pillow to his back, limped to the phone, and called his cousin. His cousin was a doctor. It was midnight. His cousin was barely awake. "I've been stabbed in the back," Chorcoran said. "What should I do?" "Find a doctor," his cousin said, and hung up. There was a hospital six minutes away. It had the best trauma center in the city. Chorcoran had met the man who ran it. He was the father of the woman Chorcoran loved. Chorcoran stumbled out to his car, wedged a pillow behind his back so he wouldn't make a mess, and set out. Halfway there, he started shaking. He stopped at a light. His hands were locked on the steering wheel. The wheel started shaking. He tried to brace himself, but the tremor went through him and shook the car. The light stayed red. He looked both ways: there was no traffic. He considered his options: he could run the light, but that was against the law; or he could wait. If he waited, though, he might black out. He'd never blacked out before. He wondered what it was like. He closed his eyes: it felt as if he was falling off a cliff. He decided he didn't want to do that. In the meantime, the light had changed. He found the hospital, drove to the emergency entrance, and parked near the door. He tried to climb out, but his legs wouldn't move. He was lucky, though: he'd arrived just as the shift was changing. Two nurses walked out and noticed him. "Can we help you?" they asked. "Yes, please," he answered in his nice boy's voice. They put him in a wheelchair and took him in.

They asked him what happened. He was embarrassed, but he told them. They looked at his back. There was a puncture wound just above his left kidney. They decided it wasn't serious. "Here's a bottle," they said. "Please urinate in it." He didn't understand, but he tried. Nothing happened. "Don't worry," they said. He was going into shock, but they didn't seem to notice. They helped him onto a table and started some IVs. He lay there and watched the drops and felt his bladder swell. He kept trying to urinate, but nothing worked. He felt his bladder getting bigger and bigger. Then his belly began to hurt.

Two police detectives arrived. They said they were there to talk to him about what happened outside his house. The pain in his belly grew worse and worse. They began to ask him questions. "Excuse me," he said. "I'm really sorry, but would it be O.K. if I asked you something?" "Sure," they said. "The man who got knifed," he said, "is he going to be O.K.?" They didn't know what he meant. "You talking about yourself?" they asked. "No," he said, "I mean . . ." "The other guy?" they asked. He nodded. "They got him in surgery," said one of the detectives. "He's got a lot of holes in him, but they think he's going to live." Chorcoran started crying then. He felt happier than he'd ever felt before. "I had this kind of epiphany," he said. "My stomach was really hurting me, but I felt so happy. I'd saved someone's life. 'Greater love hath no man' is what the Bible says. That's what I'd done. I'd laid down my life. I'd done it. Me, Tim Chorcoran, I'd finally done something good. Finally, finally. I'd done a good job. It made me so happy, I couldn't stop crying." The detectives thought he was in terrible pain. They called a nurse. She gave him a pill and he passed out. When he woke up, he felt worse than ever. That's when he said, "Please call Dr. Robbins." Robbins was the father of his girlfriend. He was a surgeon; his name was magic in the ER. Saying it saved Chorcoran's life.

When Robbins arrived, he took one look at Chorcoran and had him wheeled into surgery. The wound above his kidney led to his colon. The knife had punctured his large intestine. His belly was flooded with feces. He was septic and nearly dead. Robbins snipped and sewed, gave him a colostomy, and stapled his belly shut. They pumped him full of antibiotics and put him on morphine for three weeks. He didn't see any Chinese dragons, but he felt holy. When one of his brothers came to see 69

him, Chorcoran told him he now understood the suffering of Jesus. "He left the room crying," said Chorcoran, "but it wasn't just the morphine talking. I really
understood. God gave me the chance to learn and I did.
It nearly killed me. I almost died, but it changed my
life." It took him a year to recover. He married Robbins'
daughter, then enrolled in college.

As I listened to Chorcoran tell his story, he kept changing shapes, from Tiny Tim to the Incredible Hulk to
Christ on the Cross. I wondered how he managed to do
that. I also wondered why he needed to. One answer
turned the question back on itself: Chorcoran may have
been a changeling—not a Proteus who could control his
transformations, but an empath who, without fully re-
alizing it, became what he beheld. Sympathetic but
pliant, boyish but unformed, Chorcoran may have done
his deed simply because he'd spent seven months reading the Bible. Such an explanation implied, though, that
had he been strapped to a chair and, for seven months,
been forced to watch televised scenes of sex and violence, he would have raped and pillaged instead of saving an innocent man. In his manner, though, in his
deference to authority, his attentiveness to equals, and
his need to please, Chorcoran displayed a sweet but
malleable nature. Reading the Bible day and night may
have turned him into an Imitation of Christ, but why
he read what he read and why he read it so avidly
remained unexplained.

It took Chorcoran three days to tell me his life. On
the first day, in between the car wash and the Mexican
tomatoes, he told me all his trials and tribulations. By
the second day, he'd run out of familiar stories and
begun searching for new ones. Since he knew I was
interested and he didn't want me to be bored, he told
me a trauma he thought would please me: just after he
70 was born, he said, he'd nearly died of diarrhea.

"Really?" I said. "Oh yes," he went on, "the nurses were very worried. I was really sick. The nurses said they nearly lost me." By our third day together, Chorcoran's conscience caught up with him. He'd asked his mother, he said, and she'd corrected him: it was true he'd had some diarrhea, but he'd never come close to dying. He'd exaggerated the danger perhaps to entertain me, perhaps to dramatize himself. Not entirely true, not entirely untrue, the story of his diarrhea turned out to be just the first in a lifelong series of crises.

Until he was five, he said, his only problem was being left-handed. Then he began to have terrible nightmares. At that age, nightmares aren't uncommon, but Chorcoran's were persistent. That's when the image of Jesus first entered his life. His mother gave him a beautiful color picture of Jesus pointing to His radiant heart. Underneath His picture was a child's prayer. Chorcoran's mother told him if he said the prayer every night, Jesus would keep him safe. Chorcoran did, and so did Jesus. After that, the nuns took over. He remembered being led, in a group, down the aisle of a church. There were alcoves, and in each alcove was a dark painting. The nuns herded the children from painting to painting. "Here, children," they said, "look here": Jesus scourged, Jesus mocked, Jesus made to carry the cross, Jesus crucified. "Children," said the nuns, "can you all see?" His blood, His sorrow, His suffering. That was Chorcoran's first memory of Sunday school. His first memories of mass were extensions of his tour with the nuns: he stood beside his mother; she was very tall. He looked up at her; his eyes kept going. Stone columns rose and branched above his head. High above, the arches met and where they met they were capped with stones, round like buttons, carved like roses. The stones hung above everyone's head. Why they didn't fall, Chorcoran didn't know. People watched the priest, but Chorcoran kept his eyes on the stones. He and his mother 71 stood directly under one: "Let us pray," said the priest. So Chorcoran prayed. "Please, God," he prayed, "don't let the stones fall on my mother and me."

His mother was the moral center of the family. On weekends, she cleaned the church; on holidays, she helped the nuns at the diocese's nursing home. She was an Irish Catholic who'd borne six children and never thought of sending them anywhere but parochial school. She'd been a social worker before she was married and, once her children were old enough, she went back to it. The stories Chorcoran heard every night at dinner were her stories, heartrending tales of poor families and hungry kids.

The man she'd married, Chorcoran's dad, had been the baseball hero of her high school. He'd been the kind of ball player that a city like Cleveland produced once every few years. He'd won an athletic scholarship to Ohio State, but he liked parties more than studying, maybe even more than practice. Instead of flunking out, he let the Indians recruit him. Nothing came of it but a farm team. There he stayed until the bus rides, the motels, and the bad whiskey made him realize he was getting old before his time. He came back to Cleveland and married, if not his high school sweetheart, then one of his fans. He went to work on the line at GM, but since everyone remembered his glory days, and since he was sociable to a fault, the UAW took him in and he rose through the ranks until, by the time Chorcoran was in high school, he was the second most powerful union man in a factory of six thousand.

Chorcoran's father used alcohol. How much, Chorcoran was embarrassed to say. He did say, though, that his father threw wonderful parties. Weekends and holidays, friends and relatives filled the house and drank and joked and laughed so loud that the children fell off the couch and wet their pants. The weekend parties went on for years. Then things got mean. Chorcoran wouldn't say how mean. "He never hit my mother, though," was all he would say. Snapshots tell more: from one picture to the next, the roll of fat under his father's chin grew thicker and thicker until he looked like a grinning hippo. As Chorcoran's father waxed, his mother waned: in each picture, she grew more spare, her features more delicate, her smile more long-suffering. Chorcoran, though, couldn't have looked happier, as fat-cheeked and toothy as a chipmunk. His pictures, though, were only half true. He was ten by then, a second-born second son. By the same age, Timothy Mosher, another second-born second son, had already been cast adrift in his family's birth order. Chorcoran's experience was different but just as difficult: at the age of ten, as his father's parties grew nasty, Chorcoran began to leave home. Every weekend, Friday night and all day Saturday, he stayed at his grandfather's house. His grandfather was a very old man, a widower who kept to himself. Sometimes he and the boy would sit and talk, but most of the time Chorcoran watched TV and played alone. "That's when I started being by myself," Chorcoran said. "That's when I began being alone."

A year or two after he began leaving home, he and his family were rescued. It happened at a public park. An abandoned limestone quarry, left to fill with spring water, attracted families from all around. During the summers, Chorcoran's mother would load the kids into the old family station wagon and drive off to spend the day at the swimming hole. One day, the only parking space she could find was on the slope above the quarry. As she pulled in, her brakes failed. Slowly the car began rolling down the hill toward the water. Before it could pick up speed, it hit an old fence post, and there they stopped, six kids and their mother, jammed against a rotten piece of wood, afraid to move, calling for help. Out of nowhere, a lifeguard appeared. He was tall and blond and handsome, and he didn't say a word. Instead, he reached in and, one by one, he lifted the kids out a   73 window. Then, very gently, he opened a door and lifted Chorcoran's mother out in his arms. He set her down beside her children and smiled. "God bless you!" she said. "From the bottom of my heart!" "You bet," he said, and walked away, tall, strong, and silent, the perfect hero.

By the time Chorcoran was sixteen, being tall and strong had become very important. He was four feet ten inches when he'd entered high school, but then his hormones kicked in and in three years he shot up to five-eight. He tried out for the wrestling team and qualified as a lightweight in the 130-pound class. He wasn't the best wrestler in the world, but he was gutsy enough to be part of a team that stuck together, in season and out. In the fall, the team lifted weights; in the winter, they competed; in the summer, they rode around and picked fights. As Chorcoran explained it, the fights were all very gentlemanly, with their own set of rules: carloads of high school boys would pull up at a light and look each other over. One group would challenge the other, then lead the way to a spot off the road. Once everyone climbed out, they'd inspect each other again. People who wanted to fight, fought. People who didn't, watched. Often, the leader of one group fought the leader of the other. The rules were: equals fought equals; no weapons were allowed; a fight was over when someone surrendered.

From summer to summer, Chorcoran grew bigger and stronger and learned how to hold his own. He never grew as tall as the lifeguard in the park, but even if he had, it wouldn't have helped: when death finally caught up with him and his family, all he could do was watch. It happened when his sister was fifteen. She was two years younger than Chorcoran; she looked up to him, admired him, tagged after him. That's what she was doing when she stepped off a curb without looking. She'd been at the edge of a group, standing on a corner, her back to four lanes of fast traffic. She'd taken one

74

step back and been hit so hard she was thrown thirty feet through the air. When she came down, she was dead. There was nothing Chorcoran could have done. One second he'd been talking and laughing, the next he'd seen his sister smashed dead. For six months, he didn't cry. "I guess I was numb. I didn't know it then. All I knew was that I didn't feel anything. Then I did and I cried. My parents always said it was the beginning of the end for me. After that, I went down the tubes." Timothy Mosher had stood and watched a man drown, and, for years, carried the guilt of not helping a stranger. Ten years after Chorcoran's sister died, Chorcoran still carried her death even as he ran without looking across four lanes of traffic, fleeing the men who'd turned on him with knives. For all those years, from the moment his sister stepped off the curb to the moment he lowered his head and charged the men in the parking lot, Chorcoran did his best to stay numb. To do this, he let himself sink—not drift as Mosher had done, but sink like a leaf, settling to the bottom of a pool.

He began his descent as soon as he graduated from high school. He was accepted by a city college, but flunked out before Christmas. His father found him a job on the line at GM, lifting leaf springs onto rear axles. Each leaf spring weighed fifteen pounds; Chorcoran made thirty lifts an hour, two hundred fifty lifts a day. The entire line could have been worked by robots, but, instead, it used men who had to drink or smoke themselves stupid to do the work. Chorcoran developed his muscles while his mind switched off. He drank after work to keep it that way. He still lived at home. He'd stumble in late at night and pass out on the floor of his old bedroom. In the morning, he'd change clothes, eat breakfast, and go back to the line. He began to hate himself and everyone around him. When he wasn't asleep, drunk, or working, he thought about suicide. He survived nine months. Then he applied to a little college in Pennsylvania. The place accepted him and he left 75 home. He lasted one semester. He failed every course but American literature. That course he mastered. He read Dreiser and Steinbeck, Fitzgerald and Hemingway; he read every book on the list, but the book he loved the most was *Absalom, Absalom!* I asked him why. "Because of one of the characters," he said. "I guess I identified with him. He found out he was tainted. It was a racial thing. He realized he was one sixty-fourth black, so he went out and married a woman who looked like an orangutan. It's a parable: you find out you're tainted, so you dive into the corruption. That's how I felt about myself."

He drove back home, got drunk, and passed out in his parents' backyard. When he sobered up, his mother sat him down for a talk. "You know, Tim," she said, "you're going to be nineteen soon. That's about how old your dad was when he went off to play for the Indians." She gave him a long look. "Your father was still the life of the party back then. You're still young. It doesn't have to happen to you. You can change." He looked down at the floor. "Go see your uncle," she told him.

His uncle was his father's brother. He was the sheriff of the county. He found Chorcoran a job as a janitor in the hospital of the county jail. The place wasn't as bad as the ward in the mental hospital where Timothy Mosher had worked, but it was full of lunatics, violent lunatics locked in cages. "They screamed and rattled their bars all day," said Chorcoran. He went back to see his uncle, who called the Parks Commissioner, who obliged by finding Chorcoran another job. The job was to kill mosquitoes. Chorcoran did it for seven years, the longest he'd ever done anything.

There had never been many mosquitoes in Cleveland, but after the First War, citizens had been alarmed by tales of sleeping sickness. To prevent it, the people of Cleveland had given the Parks Department the job of

spraying, digging, and draining, year in, year out. The

Parks Department did this job good-humoredly, as if it were a grown-up ordered by a five-year-old to go out to the hallway, clap his hands, and drive away tigers. If the citizens of Cleveland wanted to pay grown men to kill mosquitoes, the Parks Department wouldn't refuse their money. The very rarity of mosquitoes, year after year, like the absence of tigers outside the bedroom door, proved the Department was doing its job. Chorcoran was hired to help.

Longtime employees of the mosquito program actually worked every day. Until politicians started calling the Parks Commissioner to find jobs for their misfit relatives, the mosquito program had just enough men and equipment, no more, no less, to do eight hours' work for eight hours' pay. The new additions changed everything: too many people on too many trucks meant not enough work to go around. Hours were rationed, distributed according to seniority. Since Chorcoran was assigned to a crew made up entirely of new men, he and they did nearly nothing. They did nearly nothing day after day, month after month, for years. "It was like this," he said. "We'd clock in at eight o'clock, sit around and have a cup of coffee. That was good for half an hour. Then we'd load the truck, sign out, and go and have breakfast. That was good for another hour, maybe an hour and a half. We went to different spots every morning. People had their favorites. They'd get into arguments sometimes. Then we'd drive to a park and smoke a couple of joints. We'd do a little work—digging, cutting, whatever. Then we'd break for lunch. Lunch took an hour. Then we'd go back and smoke another joint. We'd take a nap. And then we'd work until it was time to turn in the equipment."

For seven years, there wasn't a day Chorcoran didn't get stoned, and there wasn't a night he didn't get stoned and/or drunk. If he sobered up or straightened out, he grew anxious. He preferred to be narcotized. He could never have stayed that way if he'd still lived at home, 77 but he'd saved his pay from GM and used it to buy the little house where he was living the night he saved the man in the parking lot. Truly alone, for the first time on his own, he stopped going to mass. Instead, he began listening to preachers, late at night, on the radio.

As I listened to Chorcoran tell me about the preachers, I saw a picture in my mind: a room, heavily curtained, shaded and shuttered, darkened by a man intent on sleep. A thin shaft of light shone through a crack the man had overlooked. Not intense or focused, the light seemed brighter than it was because of the darkness of the room. Even though it was pale, the light woke the sleeping man. As Chorcoran talked on about the preachers, I began to understand the picture in my mind: the room and the man asleep in it were Chorcoran; together they constituted his life, his mind, his self. Lying in a stupor, Chorcoran heard the radio and opened his eyes. It was better to be a Christian than a Catholic, the evangelists cried. It was better to read the Bible and obey no one but Jesus, they preached. Afloat on a cloud of dope, Chorcoran experienced a religious conversion. "I decided my soul had to be saved," he said. That he worried about his soul and not his self was the result of his upbringing. As Timothy Mosher said, "Being an ex-Catholic is its own kind of religion." Whether Chorcoran called it his "soul" or his "self" didn't matter. What mattered was that he stirred to life. He started working, part-time, for Mr. Liberty, but he joined no church, attended no meetings, became part of no congregation. He stayed stoned, killed mosquitoes, listened to his radio, and typed the Bible. On his worst days, he called himself a sinner and a hypocrite. At his most sanguine, he believed there were only two pure souls in the whole world: his own and Mother Teresa's.

One Sunday afternoon, while sitting in front of Mr. Liberty's computers, he realized that if he didn't stop drinking and smoking dope and doing nothing, he'd die. In the summer of his seventh year killing mosquitoes, he cashed in all his accumulated sick leave and vacation time and went to California. An old teammate of his had moved to Los Angeles, surrendered himself to Christ, and joined a congregation. He invited Chorcoran to come out and see the light. Chorcoran decided it was time. "I was ready," he said. "I went out there to be reborn." When he arrived, his buddy said he was busy. Too busy to take him to church, too busy even to find him a place to sleep. The whole summer, Chorcoran lived in his car. He had a wonderful time. He'd wake up in the morning, drive to the beach, and read. He read remarkable books. The writings of Simone Weil, the essays and letters of Dietrich Bonhoeffer. Bonhoeffer in particular affected him. As I had with the Faulkner, I asked him why. "Sacrifice and obedience," he said. "Bonhoeffer was a Christian; he made a choice between good and evil. He plotted against Hitler and died for it. He said, 'Only those who obey can believe, and only those who believe can obey.' I'd say that to myself every day. I'd walk all the way from City Beach to Santa Monica and back and I'd be saying that to myself every step I took." He stopped smoking dope; he stopped drinking. He experienced his first epiphany. He may have simply opened his eyes again. He said he felt the Holy Spirit enter his heart. When I asked him what it was like, he gave me a tremendous grin. "It was like bathing in the ocean," he said. "It was like the finest wine." After years in a stupor, simple clarity must have felt divine.

He returned to Cleveland a new man. Unfortunately, the people who ran the mosquito program hadn't been with him for his epiphany. In his absence, they'd rearranged the work crews, promoted some people, transferred others. Every one of the airheads Chorcoran had worked with for seven years had been promoted or assigned to a better job. Everyone but Chorcoran. The bosses thought he was a fool. Chorcoran saw it as a sign, or, as he said, "the handwriting on the wall." He stayed 79 until February of the next year, then resigned. Somehow or other, he'd met a woman and fallen in love. She was studying to be a nurse. He didn't quite remember, but he thinks he met her in the library of the city college, where he'd begun to go to sit and read. She was in her last year of college and was taking a ceramics course to fill out her schedule. To be near her, Chorcoran enrolled in the course as well. Three mornings a week, he sat at a wheel and built pots. He liked centering the clay and watching it rise between his hands. He'd look up, smile at his girlfriend, and go back to his clay. The work calmed him like the best kind of occupational therapy. After being numb and alone for so long, he sat surrounded by people intent on their work, near someone he loved. For the first time in years, he began to feel his heart. That summer, he went to work, full-time, for Mr. Liberty. To occupy his evenings, he enrolled in a Bible study correspondence course. The night he rescued the man in the parking lot was the night he came fully awake.

His years of wrestling, picking fights, lifting leaf springs, and chopping brush gave him the strength and the skills to think he could do what he did. He probably didn't know the men had knives; he probably thought he could surprise and scatter them, draw them off and then escape. After years of sedation, he exploded into life. The night he looked out and saw the man in the parking lot, he was reading about hypocrites. He'd considered himself one for years. He felt guilty, not just because of what he was doing to himself, his drinking and dope smoking, but because of what he hadn't been able to do for his sister. He did what he did that night to try to make amends, not just for what he'd done in the past, but for what he hadn't. His deed, like Mosher's, was an act of self-reclamation. It gave evidence of his return to life.

He and Mosher both acted out dramas of faith in which they nearly lost their lives to gain them. In the process, they denied a secular myth: in popular fiction, heroes are all like the lifeguard who saved Chorcoran and his family. In movies and on television, in magazines and comic books, such men appear strong and self-sufficient, resourceful and self-confident. In episode after episode, they reach down and help the fallen, not because they *have* to, and not because they *need* to, but because of duty and noblesse oblige. Chorcoran and Mosher weren't fictions, though. They themselves were the fallen. They were heroes who could just as easily have been the victims. They didn't reach down, they reached up. What they dragged after them were their own souls.

CELEBRITIES

A Guardian Angel

THE FIRST Guardian Angels all worked at Mc-
Donald's. Some were griddle men; some fry cooks; Cur-
tis Sliwa, the group's founder, was an assistant manager.
This is how it happened:

Sliwa was twenty-one when he answered a Mc-
Donald's ad for a management trainee. He'd been
thrown out of prep school three weeks before graduation, then fallen through the floor of two dead-end jobs
before he applied for the position. The place that hired
him was a franchise operation in White Plains, a pleasant suburb north of New York City. Sliwa fit right in:
he was white, bright, well-spoken, and hardworking.
He also looked like he was fourteen. After four months
of learning how to make coffee and wrap hamburgers,
he was promoted to assistant night manager and assigned to the owner's other store in the Bronx. The
people who worked at the McDonald's in White Plains
referred to that store as Fort Apache. The man Sliwa
was to replace had been wounded in the line of duty.
The first thing Sliwa saw when he walked in was the
store's manager, a 260-pound Chinese named Don
Chin. Chin came vaulting over the counter, picked up 85

a customer, and threw him through the front plate-glass window. The next customer stepped up and ordered his Big Mac, shake, and fries as if nothing unusual had happened. Sliwa soon learned that nothing had: the restaurant replaced its front windows twice a month. In the Bronx, "You deserve a break today" was more than a motto.

The McDonald's Sliwa walked into was one of the few buildings in its neighborhood that weren't burnt out or boarded up. During the day, it was one of the few places that sold hot food. In the winter, it had heat; in the summer, it was air-conditioned; at night, it was lit up while everything around it was dark. No matter how poor or endangered people were, if they were young and hungry and had change in their pockets, they lined up at Mickey D's for breakfast, lunch, and dinner. The place opened early, closed late, and made a good profit. It had overhead, though. Not just windows, but health and safety. Outside, gamblers hustled games of three-card monte; inside, little pickpockets worked the customers; standing in line, the customers worked each other. Many were armed. Bumps and frowns turned into aggravated assaults. Transactions at the register were always touchy: some customers couldn't read; some couldn't add; some didn't have enough to pay; some didn't want to. To settle any and all such problems, Chin turned the stainless-steel shelf over his sandwich racks into an armory: laid out, in easy reach, were machetes, throwing stars, nun-chucks, and baseball bats. Chin had once been a member of a gang called the Savage Skulls; he had the gang's colors tattooed on his chest and back; he practiced karate, and drove to work on a motorcycle with a machete in a scabbard strapped across his shoulder blades. If he saw any sign of an argument, Chin was over the counter, bare-handed or armed, ready to fight first and ask questions later. In White Plains, people who applied for jobs were screened for good grooming, steady work habits, and an ability to learn food

preparation. In the Bronx, Chin checked criminal records, then hired for aggressiveness and loyalty. "Forget
about clean fingernails," Chin told Sliwa. "They got to
be good with their hands, and they got to be willing to
back you up. In this place, if you go over the counter,
they got to be ready to follow you. No one can handle
this alone. Here, it's one for all and all for one." Sliwa
listened and learned. Two months went by. He never
threw anyone through a window, but he learned the
Bum's Rush.

Sliwa lived in Brooklyn and took the subway back
and forth to work. On the route map of the Metropolitan
Transit Authority, the train Sliwa rode was assigned the
number 4, officially designated the Lexington Avenue
Express. Those who stayed on it into Harlem, past Yankee Stadium, into the South Bronx, had another name
for it: they called it the Mugger's Express. Once, on a
platform by Yankee Stadium, one gang attacked another with Molotov cocktails. Once, on a platform on
Jerome Avenue, a transit cop was killed by a kid with
a shotgun. The worst stretch for civilians began as the
train crossed the bend of the Harlem River. In the long
intervals between stations, the train became a trap
where small groups of armed teenaged boys moved from
car to car looking for people to rob. Night after night,
Sliwa watched the boys work: in groups of three or four,
they'd advance like skirmishers down a car, securing
exits, blocking angles of escape until they closed in on
a single victim, always the weakest, the most alone, the
easiest to frighten. The older boys would send the
youngest member of their group forward to test the victim and distract him. The little boy would ask for money
or a cigarette or the time of day; his request never mattered, only the victim's reaction: at best, fear; if nothing
else, surprise. After a few sentences, the older boys
would attack, as much for the pleasure of the victim's
pain as for his money.

Night after night, Sliwa watched. Then one night,   87

going home from work, he saw three boys close in on an old man, dressed in work clothes, snuggled up against the bulkhead by the motorman's cab sleeping off whatever he'd had to drink after work. The boys closed in as they always did; the littlest boy went forward as he usually did, but this time the victim was too tired and too drunk to hear, let alone answer the kid's questions. The boys could have turned the old man's pockets inside out and he wouldn't have noticed. But the older boys wanted to enjoy his fear. One of them broke a bottle and shoved it up under the man's jaw. The old man's eyes popped open; the boy with the bottle grinned. Sliwa couldn't stand it. "They did it right in front of me, right in front of my face." He charged them from behind. They were down and out before they knew it. The old man was crying and bleeding. The train eased into the next station. Sliwa pulled the emergency brake and waited.

Before long, a transit cop came on board. He looked at the old man; he looked at the three kids; then he looked at Sliwa. Sliwa had his McDonald's jacket and nameplate on. The cop assumed he was plainclothes or off-duty. "No, sir," said Sliwa. "I'm making a citizen's arrest." "A what?" said the cop. "Who the fuck are you?" Sliwa identified himself and repeated, "I'm making a citizen's arrest." The cop pressed the call button on his radio. "Sarge," he said, "I'm discharging this train. We got a nut case. You better come down." When the sergeant arrived, he heard Sliwa out, then handcuffed him to the three boys and took them and the old man to the police station.

The old man was too hurt and frightened to press charges. The police told Sliwa to go home and forget it. He refused. They threatened him. Sliwa persisted. He was a citizen; he'd seen a crime and stopped it; in the absence of police he had the right to detain lawbreakers. By now it was three o'clock in the morning. A lieutenant walked in: dark circles under his eyes, stubble on his chin, a paper cup of coffee steaming in his hand. They'd called him at home and woken him up for the occasion. "All right, asshole," he said. "You want to be a Boy Scout, be a Boy Scout. You got a court date along with the mutants. Don't bother going home. Arraignment's at six a.m. You're a witness. You're not there, we'll issue a warrant for you. Then it'll be your ass." Sliwa appeared and gave a statement. The boys were charged as juveniles, then released in the custody of their parents. A month passed. A trial date was set. Sliwa received a summons. He appeared to testify, but the arresting officer was otherwise occupied. Five more court dates were set; five more times Sliwa appeared to testify; each time he showed up, someone else didn't, an attorney, a defendant, an officer, until, finally, eight months later, the boys' attorneys plea-bargained the charges and the case disappeared. Sliwa kept riding the trains; the muggings continued. Sliwa sat and watched.

One night, a neighborhood lunatic walked into McDonald's with his two Dobermans, took over a booth, and dared anyone to try to throw him out. Sliwa fed the dogs Quarter Pounders; Chin tossed the man out the front door. An hour later, the police called in a $30 order. They did that every night, and every night the food was free: Chin wrote it off as insurance. That night, though, when a patrol car came for the order, Sliwa asked to be paid. The police were insulted. "What are you talking about?" they said. "We cover your ass." "Bullshit," said Sliwa. "Cash-and-carry from now on." That night, after the food crew had cleaned up and gone home, Sliwa and Chin locked the doors, turned off the lights, and talked. "Things are getting out of hand," said Sliwa. "We can take care of ourselves, but every night, I go home on the train, I see something. The cops aren't there when you need them. We got to do something." That's when Chin came up with the idea of beepers. It was 1978; only doctors, plumbers, and a few forward-thinking drug dealers carried them. Chin bought a pair in the neighborhood, and a week later, he and Sliwa began to ride the Number 4 together. This is what they did:

Sliwa sat, head down, eyes closed, in the last car, slender and baby-faced, dressed in a suit, tie, and double-breasted overcoat, the picture of an East Side yuppie who'd nodded out listening to his Walkman, so fast asleep he'd missed his stop, so dumb he didn't realize he was all alone in Indian territory. At the other end of the train stood Chin, dressed for battle, his gloves studded with rivets, his boot tips capped with steel. Chin the hunter; Sliwa the decoy. Sliwa ready to key his beeper; Chin listening for his signal. Both knew what entrapment was, so both played by the rules: Sliwa waited not just to be stalked and accosted; he waited to be surrounded, until teeth showed and fists came down. Then he hit his beeper. And then Chin came roaring from the other end of the train, crying his battle cry, whooping his war whoop, charging into the boys from behind, chopping and stomping and tossing them until the only people left standing were him and Sliwa. They waited, then, until the train neared its next stop. As it slowed into the station, Sliwa pulled the emergency brake. Chin ran as soon as the doors opened. And left Sliwa standing, pale and unsullied, surrounded by the bodies of his attackers—the only evidence of what Chin had done: the faint ripples in the steel-paneled walls of the subway car where bodies had hit and bounced off.

At first, the transit police were amazed. "You did this?" they asked, and Sliwa, as innocent as little George Washington, nodded. When his attackers woke up and claimed they'd been ambushed by a Chinese warlord, the police dismissed their stories: "You been tooting too much angel dust," they said. But Sliwa and Chin kept doing what they did, not twice, not three times, but thirty times, until, after a year of hearing the same stories, the transit police finally realized that someone was enforc-
90 ing the law without them.

The police caught up with Sliwa on a train to Rock-away. It was a train nearly empty, except for Sliwa at one end, Chin at the other, and in between, a single strung-out high school kid who made his way from car to car breaking windows with a baseball bat. As he approached Sliwa, bat in hand, Sliwa keyed his beeper, Chin came running, and decked the kid before he could do any more damage. Sliwa yanked the emergency brake; Chin ran, and Sliwa waited for the transit police. The cop who boarded didn't look surprised. He pulled the kid to his feet, shook him awake, and threw him off the train. Then he took Sliwa by the arm and marched him through the broken glass to the last car. He stood him against the train's rear window, wedged him against the bulkhead with a straight arm, and drew his revolver. At arm's length, he leveled the gun, pointed it between Sliwa's eyes. "All right, motherfucker," said the cop. "I know and you know what you been doing. So listen: this is the first time and the last time you do it on *my* train. You understand? Now get the fuck out of here." That's when Sliwa said he knew "things had gotten too personal." The next night, at McDonald's, after the food crew had cleaned up and was about to go home, Sliwa stopped them, locked the door, and sat them down. "Hey, listen, guys," he said. "I got this great idea for something we could do after work. . . ." That's how the Guardian Angels began.

There were thirteen Angels at first, mostly black and Puerto Rican kids, seventeen-year-olds who had grown up distrusting anyone who wasn't like them, kids who believed in revenge and preemptive violence, two behaviors that only perpetuated one another. Defending the Golden Arches had formed them into a working group, but out in the world, riding the trains, on their first patrols, they reverted to habit. It took two years for them to trust one another with their lives; it took just as long for them to use the martial arts Chin taught them only to defend themselves while they protected 91 others. "No drugs, no weapons, no flirting with the girls"—it was difficult for them to abide by Sliwa's rules, but by 1981 they'd coalesced into a counter-gang, an ethnically and racially mixed safety patrol, the late-adolescent equivalent of crossing guards who walked the streets and rode the trains, defending people of all ages, races, colors, and creeds against attack.

The founding of the Guardian Angels was a classic American story: begun in a restaurant whose food had become as much a symbol of America as apple pie, composed of people as racially and ethnically diverse as the clichéd American infantry platoon that fought its way from one World War II Hollywood movie to another, the Guardian Angels were a grass-roots self-defense, law-and-order organization equivalent to the posses of the Wild West, akin to the volunteer fire departments of countless American villages and towns. Better yet, the Angels were a success story appropriate to the eighties: like Apple Computer, tinkered into existence by two guys in their garage, the Guardian Angels had spread, ten years after they had begun in the Bronx, to sixty-seven cities, north and south, east and west, across the United States, Canada, and Mexico. The original thirteen had grown to 5,000. Five thousand young men, banded together to do good instead of bad, to protect and not destroy, to help and not to hurt.

The first time I heard all this, I would have stood up and cheered except I was wedged in between a desk and a giant Xerox machine squeezed into the middle room of Curtis Sliwa's wretched little apartment in New York. Sliwa was sitting opposite me, answering two phones with multiple lines, as well as responding to CB radio messages broadcast to him by Guardian Angels on patrol in midtown Manhattan. To the Angels who radioed him, he answered as "Rock" or "Angel 1." To telephone callers he knew, he answered as "Curtis." To strangers, he pretended to be a well-meaning but ignorant office employee. It was the spring of 1988, just before a Hollywood movie about street gangs in LA, a movie called *Colors*, was to be released. Sliwa had publicly protested the film as equivalent to yelling "Fire!" in a crowded theater. Half the calls he received were from out-of-town journalists who wanted to interview him about the movie; the rest of the calls were from local reporters, press, radio, or TV who wanted to know about street gangs. Sometimes Sliwa spoke didactically, sometimes polemically; sometimes he spoke in a colloquial way, sometimes in a formal fashion. Calls came in rapidly, in batches, like calls to the desk of a commodities broker, and as he answered each call, Sliwa changed his voice as well as his persona. On the phone lines, he was six different people; responding to the frantic, garbled bursts of the CB radio, he was two more; all the time, he conducted himself as if he were in an office rather than next door to his own kitchen. In the midst of this, he spoke with me, telling the story of the Guardian Angels, stopping and starting exactly where he left off to talk with a reporter from Indianapolis or an anchorwoman from WNBC. Speaking to me, he imitated the voices and gestures and accents of all the major actors in the Angels' story: Chin vaulting the counter, the lunatic with his Dobermans, the old man asleep on the train, the three boys who attacked him, the transit cop radioing his sergeant, the grizzled lieutenant with his coffee cup, on and on, one set of voices, faces, and gestures after another, all interrupted by phone calls and radio chatter while I sat and watched and listened and wondered if I was talking to an ordinary man or a multiple personality, to a social activist or a stand-up comic who did imitations. It took Sliwa four hours to tell me how he founded the Guardian Angels; then he broke off, explaining he had an appointment with a TV talk show, followed by a private screening of *Colors*, arranged by the studio that produced it. Sliwa wasn't the first public personality I'd   93 ever talked to, but I'd never seen anyone shift back and forth between selves so rapidly or effortlessly. People like Sliwa, with many roles and many responsibilities, always change to suit the occasion, but Sliwa was more of a chameleon than anyone I'd ever met. As I left his apartment, I wondered how and why he'd become so skilled at changing himself to imitate and accommodate others. I'd been entertained by his stories, but I still didn't understand why he'd put himself at risk riding the trains with Chin, or even how he'd come to work at McDonald's in the first place. How all this was—or wasn't—related to his ability to impersonate others, I hoped to discover when I saw him the next day.

Sliwa's "next day" began before dawn in the rain on the sidewalk outside the apartment of a young man of good family named Chambers, who'd been on trial for murdering a young woman of equally good family named Levin; the two had been lovers; they'd engaged in sex in the park behind the Metropolitan Museum of Art; in the process the young woman may or may not have done something unpleasant to Chambers, and the young man had killed her, perhaps by accident, perhaps not. Chambers' trial had been a media circus; Sliwa, his wife, and a crowd of Angels had become part of the parade both because Sliwa believed Chambers was guilty and because the TV crews occasionally turned their cameras from the trial to the Angels' daily demonstrations against rape. Chambers' jury had reached a verdict in the middle of the night and Sliwa had driven a panel van of Angels to Chambers' house to picket and then follow him to the courthouse to hear his fate. By the time the Chambers jury had announced its guilty verdict, and Sliwa had been one of the many interested observers interviewed on the courthouse steps, it was two in the afternoon, Sliwa was soaked to the skin and had been giving interviews alternating with orders for twenty hours. At three o'clock I met him at his apartment; he changed clothes, drank a cup of coffee, and

94

we drove off in the same van that had hounded Chambers to his conviction. This time, the van drove to an old brownstone in a crack neighborhood. The landlord had given the Angels a free apartment in return for their patrolling his street. The Angels had turned the narrow basement apartment into a bunkhouse, where one patrol slept while another walked the streets, prepared to detain any drug dealers they met. For the next four hours, I drank coffee and listened, while down the hall four young Angels slept and snored, and Sliwa sat across a table from me, impersonating the principal players in his life.

Sliwa was a middle child, but unlike Timothy Mosher, the taxi driver, who'd been cast adrift in his family's birth order, Sliwa was at the center of his, born between two girls, his older sister born seven years before him, his younger sister born one year after. As an only son, Sliwa was treated as a first-born male, not just nurtured by his mother, but also coddled by his older sister. For fathers, Sliwa had two, one his own, the other his mother's; one Polish-American, the other Italian; one a merchant seaman, a devoted man, but more absent than present; the other an old saddlemaker turned junk collector who lived in Sliwa's house. Sliwa's own father, the Pole, loved his family, but his voyages were long and distant. When he returned, he brought back sea chests full of treasures, but his treasures were books, not doubloons, books of every kind, picture books and story books, history books and geography books, books collected from Seamen's Missions all over the globe and hauled back to the family house in Canarsie, unloaded in the basement, stacked in piles, crammed on shelves, a hoard of knowledge. Year after year, Sliwa's father was the absent man who returned with stories of distant places and strange worlds, but morning and night, it was Sliwa's grandfather, the old Italian, who sat across the dining-room table from him and told tales about his own suffering and survival. When Sliwa was in the 95 fourth grade, he began to read his father's books and the world beyond Brooklyn opened to him, but long before he could read and long after he'd learned how, it was his grandfather's stories that filled his life.

His grandfather came from Andria, on the Adriatic, just above the heel of the boot. He'd grown up in a mud hut dug into a hillside. "That's what it means to be dirt poor," his grandfather had said. The woman he loved came from a family much better than his. Every night he played his guitar outside her window and sang songs of love. One night, she climbed down and they eloped. They hid in a huge wine barrel in a basement. For two months, her family searched for her, and for two months, the lovers hid in the barrel. When, at last, they climbed out, Sliwa's grandmother was pregnant. Bitterly, her family accepted her marriage. In 1921, Sliwa's grandparents set sail for America. Sliwa's mother was conceived on the high seas.

In America, they lived in great poverty. They had fourteen children and never enough food. Over and over, Sliwa's grandfather told the same stories. "A single apple," he'd begin, and as Sliwa spoke to me, he became his grandfather, holding a single green apple, cupped in his fingers like a Fabergé egg, turning it left, turning it right, admiring it, studying it. In his left hand, he held the apple; in his right, a knife. All around him stood his children. Slowly, he turned the apple. All day, Sliwa's grandfather cut leather. His eyes were keen, his knife like a razor. He traced the first curve down the green skin, barely breaking it. His children watched. He traced the second curve. He held the apple at arm's length, brought it close to him again, and, satisfied that his lines were true and the portion just, he sliced through the skin and cut the first wedge. He would cut thirteen more, one at a time, one for each child, and with every slice he would tell a story, a special story that suited each child and his portion, so that to carve an apple and feed it to everyone would take Sliwa's grandfather two hours.

"Coal!" the old man would begin again, and, once more, Sliwa turned into his grandfather, not hoary and bent, but tall and stern. One winter, they were too poor to buy coal. Every day, the children followed the coal carts, waiting and waiting, standing at a distance, trembling and waiting for chunks of coal to tumble off onto the street. Days went by, trailing the carts, and no coal fell. Then, one day, a few chunks tumbled off and the children brought them home to the kitchen. When Sliwa's grandfather saw what they had done, he rose like a prophet in his wrath and he beat them with his belt, harder than he'd ever whipped them before. "Thieves!" he called them. Thieves they were: the coal wasn't theirs; the coal was stolen. There was no place in his house for things that belonged to others. They had disgraced him. They had disgraced themselves. And so the chunks of coal remained on the kitchen table, black, unburned and untouchable, gazed at by the children as they passed from one frozen room to another.

Two of the children caught rheumatic fever. Sliwa's grandfather held them and watched and listened as they heaved, rattled, and died. There was nothing he could do: he had no money for doctors. Then Sliwa's mother caught the fever. By then, the Depression had begun, and Sliwa's grandfather had found work digging ditches for the WPA. Two miles he walked to work and two miles back, no money for carfare. One day, Sliwa's mother grew worse. Her father came home from work, saw she was dying, put her on his back, and carried her six miles to a special hospital, talking and joking all the way, telling her stories and making her laugh so she'd live long enough to reach the clinic. There, the nurses took her in and there she stayed for a year.

By the time Sliwa's mother had married and raised a family of her own, Sliwa's grandmother had died, and

Sliwa's grandfather had grown very old. He lived until he was ninety-nine, and until the morning he couldn't get out of bed, he worked. Age bent him double; cataracts blinded him; arthritis froze his hands into mittens, but every morning, he pulled a cart through the streets, collecting scrap metal and hauling it to a junkyard to sell. He began and ended every working day with the same meals, meals that marked the hours like church bells, meals he took like sacraments in memory of all the times he'd had nothing to eat. To begin each day the old man broke an egg into his cup. Sliwa did as he did: cracked it on the rim, then added coffee. Then, spoon perfectly vertical, thumb and finger held high on the handle, he stirred and stirred and stirred, his hand transcribing an orbit above the cup, until, head back, elbow out, he raised the cup and quaffed it like ale from a tankard. That was all he ate or drank for the rest of the day until he'd filled his cart, hauled his scrap, and collected his money. Then it was time for his afternoon meal. He sat at the table and waited to be served, as grave as a bishop listening for the trumpet of a Te Deum. Every meal began with lamb: two shoulder chops, perfectly trimmed and perfectly broiled; then a salad of escarole, not a single leaf blemished or bruised; to one side, a quarter loaf of bread, no more, no less, and, in front, a single glass of wine. As he sliced the meat, broke a piece of bread, raised the wine to his lips, each gesture was precise, each morsel savored, every bite restored his strength. Only when he finished did he talk. "He could imitate anyone," said Sliwa, "past or present, a guy on the street or someone he hadn't seen in fifty years. Just listening to him, he taught me how to tell a story." But Sliwa's grandfather taught him more than that: a mimic doesn't just remember something, he ingests it; he doesn't just retell it, he re-creates it. When Sliwa's father returned from a voyage, he told stories to explain the world. When Sliwa's grandfather finished his dinner, 98 he told stories to encompass it. Sliwa learned well.

Twenty-five years later, it was wonderful to watch him imitate his grandfather. Still, I wondered why he'd been such a good student.

The room where Sliwa's grandfather ate and talked was in a house in a neighborhood where Sliwa wasn't just a kid but somebody's nephew and someone else's cousin. Even with an absent father, his boyhood should have been secure. But for the first two years of his life, and for the first nine years of his mother's marriage, he and his older sister and their mother lived in exile, in a four-story house lodged with three generations of Polish relatives, trapped in a Polish neighborhood in Chicago, his father's hometown. They were there because Sliwa's father was away at sea, but they were left all alone, Italians among Poles, dark-haired kids among blonds, spaghetti eaters in a land of dumplings, wops, dagos, outsiders.

When, at last, the family moved to their own home in Canarsie, his Italian cousins made fun of his name: " 'Sliwa'?" they'd say. "What kind of name is 'Sliwa'?" A wop among Poles, Sliwa became a Polack among Italians. School made things worse: the Catholic elementary school in his neighborhood changed from all white to nearly all black the year Sliwa began first grade. The kid who'd been an Italian among Poles became nearly the only white in his class. He also became a source of lunch money for bullies. For four years, older boys ambushed him. He jumped fences, ran down alleys, scampered through backyards, but day after day, they laid traps for him, until, finally, when he was ten, he developed ulcers and an inflamed appendix. At school, he tried to excel; on the streets, he tried to escape; at home, he was too proud to confess how scared he was. Only after the doctors removed his appendix did he break down and tell his mother about the bullies. For four weeks, he stayed home, recovering from the surgery. He read his father's books and thought about the wide world, while his mother decided how to help 99 him. The first thing she did was enroll him in a public school. The second thing she did was enroll him in a judo class. His father had learned judo years before on a voyage to Hawaii, but he'd never taught his son, afraid he'd become a bully like the sons of his friends who'd learned "the gentle art" from their fathers. For the next four years, Sliwa learned judo. The night he walked into the McDonald's in the Bronx, he knew how to defend himself. Because of his mother, Sliwa never ran from bullies again.

Not that there were any at his new school: almost all his classmates were Jews. The lone white kid among blacks became the Gentile among Jews. Worse yet, the Jews were smarter and worked harder than any kids he'd ever known. "This was fifth, sixth grade," Sliwa said, "and these kids, they'd spend the whole night in the New York Public Library, *reading*. Plus, they could *talk*. They'd talk; they'd argue; they were articulate; they'd write essays full of footnotes. I had to run hard to keep up." He began to spend weekends in his basement reading his father's treasures. Outside on the street, his cousins played stickball and made remarks. "Yo, Curt! Where you been, man? How come you been reading all the time? You turning into some kind of brainiac, some kind of Jew boy? Come on, man, play some ball." After that, Sliwa began to budget his time: half a day Saturday outside, playing ball; half a day inside, reading; half a day being "normal" like his cousins; half a day being a brainiac to compete in school.

Sliwa's older sister attended a Catholic girls' school. She was on the debating team there. She introduced her brother to her coach. Her coach also taught at a Catholic boys' school called Brooklyn Prep. In the 1960s, Brooklyn Prep was considered one of the finest parochial boys' schools in the New York area. The sons of the sons of graduates of Brooklyn Prep attended the school, went on to the best colleges, were accepted by the most prestigious professional schools, and returned to New York to become eminent physicians and distinguished attorneys. Whether it was Sliwa's mother and father, or Sliwa's mother and older sister, or all of them, someone in Sliwa's family decided he was destined for a brilliant professional career. Sliwa's sister pleaded his case to her coach, and her coach pleaded his case to the headmaster of the school, a Jesuit named John Alexander, a wiry, street-smart, sharp-eyed, and skeptical priest who looked as hard and dark as a piece of finished mahogany. To one side, at one end of a conference table, sat Sliwa, his mother, and his father. The debating coach stood next to them like a defense attorney beside his clients. At the other end of the table sat Alexander, chain-smoking Pall Malls, rubbing the back of his neck, shaking his head from side to side as the debating coach lobbed one eloquent plea after another at him. "I don't know; I don't know," Alexander kept muttering as the coach delivered what Sliwa said was "the equivalent of the Gettysburg Address." When it was over, Sliwa was accepted without the need for entrance exams, exams everyone knew he would have failed even though he was enrolled in advanced placement courses in public school. His admission was special and provisional, more the result of the debate coach's eloquence than the headmaster's confidence.

Sliwa entered prep school as much an outsider as ever, a Brooklyn kid in a school full of Westchester and Long Island suburbanites; the child of second-generation immigrants among the children of Irish-American gentry; the son of parents who worked with their hands to pay his tuition (his mother, a dental technician; his father come ashore to work as a cabinetmaker) enrolled with the offspring of women who did nothing but shop and men who lifted nothing heavier than a pen or a scalpel. Year after year, in school after school and place after place, Sliwa had been in the minority, the wrong nationality, the wrong race, the wrong religion, and now, the wrong class. He had survived black bullies, 101 endured his cousins, competed with Jews; now he had to prove himself to a skeptical headmaster and learn to live with rich boys. As I sat and watched Sliwa impersonate the Rev. John Alexander, S.J., I thought of all the gauntlets he'd run to reach Brooklyn Prep. As Sliwa hunched forward, smoking an imaginary Pall Mall, rubbing the back of his neck, I realized why he'd become such a good mimic: he'd done it to survive.

Every morning before school, Sliwa delivered papers for the *Daily News*. He began to notice the trash along his route, and as he emptied his wagon of newspapers, he began to fill it with debris. Soon he began to go out every day after school to clean the streets. His grandfather scavenged in the morning; Sliwa began to pick trash in the afternoon. He found five abandoned shopping carts, roped them together, and pulled them up and down the streets, collecting cans, bottles, and old newspapers. All this garbage he brought home. In his front yard, he separated the trash into piles, glass in one, cans pounded flat in another, newspapers bundled and stacked in a third. The piles began to grow. Neighbors objected, but Sliwa's parents didn't stop him. The piles became hillocks. Sliwa called commercial carting companies. They wouldn't come for anything less than five and a half tons. He kept collecting trash. His neighbors grew angrier. His cousins called after him, "Hey, Curt, you turning into a 'junkie'?" It was 1969, a time when people first began to talk of "Spaceship Earth"; a time when the word "Environment" began to be written with capital letters, when pollution and overpopulation first became national and then international political issues. Sliwa's grandfather picked scrap for the same reason nineteenth-century Italian immigrants picked rags: for the poorest of the poor, garbage was money. Sliwa was paid $65 for the first load of trash hauled from his front yard. As soon as it was gone, he collected more, until, after two years of picking and sorting, pounding and piling, he'd accumulated eighty

A Guardian Angel

tons of the stuff and earned $950. At that rate of return, Sliwa wasn't scavenging the streets of his neighborhood to make money.

I didn't ask and Sliwa didn't explain why he cleaned the streets for two years. He didn't explain, perhaps because he thought the environmental reasons for what he did were obvious enough. I didn't ask for two reasons: first, the idea of a fifteen-year-old boy turning his front yard into a garbage dump was so preposterous I couldn't decide if what he'd done was a virtue or a vice, and second, because he quickly launched into a dramatic description of how, one winter morning, he'd saved six people from a burning building. That story, later confirmed with news clippings worthy of a Carnegie Hero Fund Medal, will soon follow, complete with its own puzzlements. For now, consider the reasons for Sliwa's passionate trash collecting:

One reason was the example of his grandfather. Not just what the old man did each morning, but what he did each summer: in the backyard, he grew tomatoes. His sight was so poor, he weeded his garden by touch alone, patting the earth, winnowing it, plucking out weeds and stones, nails and bottle caps, grooming the soil, sifting it inch by inch until the earth was pure. For the same reason the old man would touch no stolen coal, he picked his garden clean. Purity, cleanliness, and control—those were some of the reasons Sliwa cleaned the streets. He tended his neighborhood the way his grandfather tended his garden.

Another reason had to do with his father: for twenty years, Sliwa's father had sailed the globe. The color photographs of the earth made by orbiting astronauts, the "big blue marble" pictures that became book covers and wall posters, those transcendent overviews invoked an understanding that Sliwa's father had himself achieved after dozens of voyages, an understanding that he taught his son with books and stories every time he came home. By cleaning the streets and recycling his 103 pickings, Sliwa combined his father's overview with the rootedness of his grandfather.

All that considered, there still remains the question of Sliwa's passion: trying to clean a big city neighborhood like Canarsie, five shopping carts at a time, was like trying to clean the Augean stables with a push broom. Sliwa's parents may have supported him, but his relatives made fun of him and his neighbors became angry. Why did he single-handedly persist? Did he think he was a Little Dutch Boy holding back the ocean with his thumb? What was he trying to prove? The answer to that is also the answer to why, a year after he entered Brooklyn Prep and began cleaning Canarsie, he ran into a burning building to save six people.

It happened before dawn, three days before Christmas 1970. Sliwa was folding newspapers, rolling rubber bands around them, getting ready to set out on his paper route. He was all alone, standing by the window of an unheated storefront the *Daily News* used as a drop point. Head down, half awake, folding each paper, banding and stowing it, Sliwa heard two muffled booms: "Boom-boom," he said to me, and hit the table with his fists. Boom-boom, like the sound of someone in the next room hitting a drum. He heard it and looked up but no one was there. He went back to his papers. Then: boom-boom. He looked outside. His dog was chasing squirrels through the snow. He could see the dog's breath. The sky was still dark. He went back to his papers. Then again: boom-boom. This time when he looked, he saw smoke, faint, white against white, drifting through the air, and as he kept looking, he saw little orange flames licking up under the eaves of a wooden tenement down the block.

He ran as fast as he could. The building was burning. He put his shoulder against the door. Sliwa wasn't a big kid. The door wouldn't budge. The boom-booms had been the sounds of doors and doorframes expanding and cracking in the heat. Sliwa ran at the door and slammed into it; ran at the door and slammed into it. As he stood there panting, shoulder against it, the door blew off its hinges, exploded outward by the smoke and heat. Sliwa and the door sailed across the street and skidded through the snow, the door aflame along its edges, Sliwa on his back, stunned, looking up at where the door had been, now a rectangle of orange flames and smoke, huge tongues of flame jetting into the night air. His dog let out a howl and ran home. Sliwa pulled himself up, stood there looking at the flames, then went in. In a room to the right, an old man sat, naked, in a chair. "Come on! Come on!" shouted Sliwa. The old man waved him away. "No clothes. I got no clothes." Sliwa took off his Army coat, wrapped it around the old man, and dragged him out. He went in again, pounded on the door across the hall and led out a young couple. Then in again, up a flight, just as another young couple with a child came stumbling down. He led them out, then went up the stairs again, into the rear apartment. Its walls were on fire. Sitting on the bed, he saw what looked like a wax candle shaped like a person, except it wasn't a candle, it was an old woman and she was melting. She was very old. She'd grown senile. For years, she'd threatened to set fire to herself. Early that morning, she had. Sliwa stumbled down the stairs, out into the air, his eyebrows singed, his hair scorched, his face blackened; he sat on the curb, stunned by the heat, shivering and coughing. Then, without thinking, he stood up, walked back to his storefront, collected his papers, loaded his wagon, and began his route. He'd delivered 125 papers by the time the police found him and took him to the hospital.

The *Daily News* declared him a hero. The mayor of New York presented him with a plaque; the *Canarsie Courier* ran his picture and his story; the *New York Sunday News* featured him with his family. Richard Nixon granted him a photo opportunity as part of National Newspaperboy Day. His mother started a scrapbook:

Curt Sliwa, Newsboy Hero/Curt Sliwa, Environmental
Crusader/Curt Sliwa, Model Citizen. After the fact,
the rewards for being a hero were obvious: his cousins
shut up; his neighbors quieted down; no one called him
a Polack or stole his lunch money. At school, he was
elected to the Student Council. All that came after he
ran into the burning building. But why did he do it?
He had never been as unhappy or frustrated as Tim
Mosher, the taxi driver, or as aimless and guilt-ridden
as Tim Chorcoran, the Little Tailor turned into the Incredible Hulk. Still, there were some similarities: Chorcoran did what he did right after reading St. Matthew;
Sliwa, a Catholic boy enrolled in a Jesuit school, risked
his life three days before Christmas. Sliwa was no emotional cripple, but he had developed ulcers and had his
appendix removed after four years of running from bullies, and he had been, even after entering Brooklyn
Prep, the "odd man out," what sociologists call "lim-
inal," on the edge, teetering on the line, a kid with his
nose pressed against the glass, an outsider looking in.
His mother and his older sister adored him, but his
father was too often absent. He lived in a family neighborhood, but he had a peculiar last name. A member
of the majority, he was treated like a minority. Half
strange, half familiar; half strong, half weak; half secure, half vulnerable—Sliwa was a kid with a fault line
down his center. The tension between his halves and
the need to resolve that tension impelled him to act. To
save lives and cleanse the world, to act rather than be
acted upon, to deny weakness by displaying strength,
to prove he was ordinary by doing something extraordinary—the push and pull of these motives, like the rods
and linkages of an engine, propelled him to act. The
ideals he served were pure and powerful: harmony and
balance, health and safety, order and cleanliness—they
were all elements of a classic triad, all forms of the
Good, the True, and the Beautiful. Model Citizen, not
106　mixed-blood hyphenate; Newsboy Hero, not victim; En-

vironmental Crusader, not follower—to all this, Sliwa
aspired, not because it was so distant but because, for
years, it had been just beyond his reach.

At school, Sliwa ended his junior year in glory, so
admired by one and all that he was elected president
of the Student Council. Success went to his head. In his
senior year, he tested his strength. Outside of school,
he took on four members of a street gang and won. In
school, he took on his headmaster and lost. The fight
with the gang members happened on a school day during lunch at a delicatessen. Brooklyn Prep was located
in Crown Heights, an area settled by Hasidic Jews, but
also inhabited by blacks and Hispanics whose gangs
often harassed the Hasids, both because they were Jews
and because they were outsiders. Synagogues were van-
dalized; Yeshiva students were ambushed and beaten;
shops were pilfered. The Hasids organized street
watches and citizens' patrols to defend themselves, but
the gangs were quick and unpredictable, and although
the patrols were a deterrent, they couldn't be everywhere at once. When four members of a Hispanic gang
called the Tomahawks entered a deli near Brooklyn
Prep, the only people who could have stood between
them and the man and wife who ran the deli were a
crowd of Brooklyn Prep seniors on their lunch break.
The Tomahawks swept into the deli like Indians attacking a ranch. "We're gonna burn ya! We're gonna
burn ya! *Sieg Heil! Sieg Heil!*" they yelled. The owners
backed away from the counter; the Brooklyn Prep students didn't move. One Tomahawk pulled Jewish or-
naments off the wall; another knocked over a display of
canned goods; another threw cakes and cookies on the
floor and ground them to a pulp. Half the Brooklyn
Prep football team had gone to the deli for lunch. As
the Tomahawks took the place apart, linemen and line-
backers sat and watched. Sliwa walked in late. One of
the Tomahawks punched him in the side of the head
with a rivet-studded glove. Sliwa hadn't practiced judo

for three years, but the sight of his own blood made him react. He swept one Tomahawk through the deli's front window. The shattered glass sliced open the back of another. The two who were left ran. The glass and blood brought the Brooklyn Prep football team off the bench. They jumped on the two wounded Tomahawks and held them until the police arrived. Sliwa's exploit didn't make the papers, but his reputation at school grew even greater: Curt Sliwa, Protector of the Weak/Curt Sliwa, Defender of Justice.

Sometime around Easter, Sliwa squared off against the Rev. John Alexander. At issue was the school's dress code. Sliwa should have known the outcome of the argument in advance, but a year of single-handed victories had impaired his judgment. Brooklyn Prep was run like many Jesuit schools: in class, argument and debate were encouraged. No subjects were forbidden; no discussion foreclosed. During class, any and all intellectual disagreements were permitted. But once the bell rang, orders were orders; authority was obeyed. The disagreement between the school's headmaster and the school's Student Council president soon became a power struggle. "It got out of hand," said Sliwa. "It was like a chem lab experiment that got out of control." Except it was Sliwa that burned down: three weeks before graduation, Alexander threw him out of school. Earlier that year, Alexander had expelled a half dozen other seniors, varsity athletes and whiz kids, all for using drugs. Rules were rules. Break them and suffer the consequences. Sliwa had pushed too hard and, once again, he'd become an outsider looking in. His expulsion was the worst misfortune he'd suffered since he'd broken down running from bullies when he was ten. For seven years, he'd fought his way to a place of eminence. The last two years of his life had seemed to confirm everything he dreamed he deserved. Sliwa was the classic 98-pound weakling who'd grown tired of people kicking sand in his face: he'd sent away to Charles Atlas, done his exercises, and built himself into a Man of Muscle. Everyone admired him; no one laughed at him anymore. But then—he took on someone too big for him. He was thrown off the beach. He had to start all over again.

He refused to attend the local public high school. His parents said, "Fine. You owe us room and board. Get a job." Sliwa found one as the attendant of an all-night gas station on the edge of his neighborhood. The job came with the title of "night manager" and a salary of $170 per week, $70 of which Sliwa paid to his parents. The station was the only one around open all night and the last place in the neighborhood people could buy gas before the Parkway. During the day, it employed a mechanic, but at night the garage doors were locked and the register emptied. Motorists pumped their own gas and paid exact change. The only thing Sliwa had to do—the only thing he could do—was take their money and drop it into a locked floor safe. A sign on the window said it all: "Exact Change. Attendant Has No Key." No one ever read the sign. Desperate people coasted in with broken fan belts, flat tires, and busted radiators. "Can't help you," said Sliwa. "The mechanic's gone. The doors are locked." Sometimes the people would plead, sometimes they'd threaten, sometimes they'd weep. Punks would drive in, fill up, and speed off without paying. Sometimes Sliwa recorded their license-plate numbers, sometimes not. The only people he could help were the lost souls who drove in asking for directions. Every morning at sunrise, a man named Pedro would arrive with a key to check the total-gallons-pumped against the money in the floor safe. Pedro had a ritual: first business, then pleasure; first money, then coffee. Not just any coffee, but Café Bustelo, black and fragrant, brewed exactly and sipped reverently. "Medicine for my soul," he'd say, then stir his cup like Sliwa's grandfather. He'd drink, then he'd talk. He'd talk about food and shelter. He'd talk about having enough money left 109 at the end of the month to buy his kid a box of disposable diapers. Everything he said reminded Sliwa of what he'd taken for granted: food to eat, a place to sleep, a little money left for a tiny luxury; Pedro's stories could have been the stories of Sliwa's grandfather, stories Sliwa had forgotten until he himself had hit bottom and woken up listening to Pedro muse about Pampers.

The first month Sliwa worked the job, he was robbed. Three men came in, one with a shotgun. They opened the till. "Where's the money?" "It's in the floor safe," Sliwa said. "Then open the fuckin' safe." "I can't," said Sliwa, "I don't have the key." They jammed the shotgun under his chin. "Open the fuckin' safe." Sliwa had trouble talking with a gun under his jaw. "I can't," he said. "You better learn how or you ain't gonna have shit for brains." "I don't have the key," he said. They put both barrels in his ear and cocked the hammers. "You don't have the key, then use your fingernails. Get down and open the goddamn safe." Sliwa went down on his knees. They put the shotgun behind his head and kept pushing until his forehead touched the floor. They eased off the hammers, then cocked them again. "O.K., chickenshit, get to work. We want to hear you scratch." Years later, when Sliwa rode the trains with Chin, he'd listen to the boys as they closed in around him. Now and then, one would say to the others: "I want the smell, man. I want the smell." Sliwa knew what that meant: the smell of a victim, so frightened, he lost control of his bladder or his bowels. They wanted the smell of a man so frightened he became a child. That night in the gas station, the guys with the gun did that to Sliwa. They took everything that wasn't bolted down and left him on the floor. The next morning, he didn't quit. He worked two more years. It took him that long to recover. It had been twelve years since bullies first ambushed him. Twelve years and one night, then they'd done it again.

How Sliwa found his next job, he didn't explain. Compared with babysitting a gas station, it was a step up in the world, but it was still a night job, as isolated and obscure as Tim Mosher's taxi driving. What Sliwa did was restock an A&P after hours, part of a crew that worked through the night like elves who disappeared before shoppers entered the store the next morning. Sliwa began as a general merchandise clerk, but after a few months of not breaking anything, he was given responsibility for a single aisle. In the language of the grocery business, Sliwa was put in charge of a "glass aisle," a corridor six feet high and a hundred feet long, row after row of products, some in bottles, some in jars, all in glass. Sliwa worked on his aisle as painstakingly as his grandfather had once cleaned his garden, as obsessively as Sliwa himself had once scoured his neighborhood. Night after night, he dusted and shined and straightened, restructuring shelf after shelf, until one morning, when the sun shone down Sliwa's aisle, the whole aisle lit up with rainbows cast by prisms that until then had been nothing but bottles of cooking oil and corn syrup. The store's manager was so astonished he made photographs of the display for his own records, and when the rainbows returned, morning after morning, hired a photographer to take pictures to be sent to A&P headquarters in New Jersey.

The glass aisle gave evidence of Sliwa's love of order, cleanliness, and detail. Its perfection won him his first promotion, from clerk to "key man," a job equivalent to foreman, its title bestowed on an employee considered trustworthy enough to lock and unlock a store in the absence of a manager or an assistant manager. Midway between workers and managers, a key man made sure that orders were carried out, that shelves were stocked, items marked, logbooks kept, and inventories filled. "What a key man did," said Sliwa, "was kick ass. He got grief coming and going. He got grief from the union for being management's stooge, and he got grief from the bosses every time someone screwed up." It was a job for a self-contained, self-directed person who believed more in doing something well than in being liked. Sliwa did the job the way he'd collected trash: single-handedly and compulsively. He worked hard, then he worked harder. He did his job so well that the men he directed despised him. One day, in the warehouse, Sliwa fell from a lift. He broke two bones in his wrist and one in his elbow. He lay on the floor and screamed. The men in his crew stopped what they were doing. They stopped and looked, then went back to work. They would have paid more attention to a packing case. The produce manager took Sliwa to the hospital. The doctors put his arm in a cast and told him he'd have to wear it for three months. Two days later, Sliwa cut the cast off and went back to work. He did everything he did before, but he did it one-handed. The slightest movement caused him pain. Sliwa kept working.

Management took note. The Great Atlantic and Pacific Tea Company had fallen on hard times. A few years more and it would be sold, then resold, until it finally fell into the hands of a German conglomerate. But at the moment Sliwa returned to work, single-handedly reprising his role as the Little Dutch Boy, A&P corporate management began to close stores and cut its work force. That corporate policy manifested itself for Sliwa's benefit in the form of a promotion, or at least the offer of a promotion: there was a store, Sliwa was told; it was an unprofitable store; it was unprofitable because its manager wasn't pulling his weight. The company was going to close the place and fire the manager. Unless, of course, Sliwa wanted the man's job. Then the company would just fire the man and not close the store until Sliwa had a chance to try to save it. If Sliwa wanted the challenge, the job was his. Sliwa asked if he could inspect the store before he made up his mind. What he saw when he went there surprised him: the place was well run. It was losing money, not because of its manager, but because of its neighborhood. The manager couldn't have run the place better if he'd owned it himself. The manager's kids bagged groceries; the manager's wife answered the phone. The manager himself didn't just wear an A&P apron: he wore an A&P shirt, an A&P hat, an A&P nametag. He was so devoted to the company, Sliwa imagined he wore A&P underwear and slept between A&P sheets. He'd worked for A&P for twenty years. The only reason Sliwa could think of for firing him was to avoid paying his retirement benefits. Sliwa declined the promotion. His boss called him an "ungrateful asshole." The company gave Sliwa two weeks' notice. Shunned by everyone, workers and management alike, Sliwa went looking for a new job. What he found was the McDonald's in White Plains.

McDonald's taught him teamwork. Not the sham corporate ideology that imposed control from above by demanding homogeneity from everyone below. And not a set of assembly-line work rules practiced by food crews whose members had to depend on one another to produce a finished product for a waiting customer. Chin, the night manager, ex-gang member, taught Sliwa teamwork: "No one can handle this alone. Here it's one for all and all for one." Until then, Sliwa had done everything alone. He'd saved lives, cleaned streets, and won praise, but he'd remained solitary, and by the time he reached A&P, he'd become an outcast again, a condition he'd suffered since he was old enough to go to school. At the McDonald's in the Bronx, he became part of a diverse whole.

As Sliwa sat across from me in the basement apartment the Angels had turned into a bunkhouse, he added something to the story he'd told me the day before about how the Angels began: a year after he started working in the Bronx—about the time he and Chin began riding the Mugger's Express—Sliwa organized his food crew into a cleanup brigade. Every Saturday, sixteen of them, led by Sliwa, picked trash off the main shopping street of the Bronx. The *Daily News* wrote a story about them. The head of the Bronx Chamber of Commerce, the 113 borough president, a city councilman, a state assemblyman, the governor of New York, and a U.S. congressman wrote Sliwa letters of commendation. Once again, Sliwa played Mr. Environmental Crusader, but this time he did it with sixteen others. He was their leader, but he worked side by side with them. From that group of McDonald's street cleaners, Sliwa recruited the first thirteen Guardian Angels. Cleaning streets and saving lives formed a pattern that Sliwa had enacted and then reenacted since he was fifteen. He was twenty-two when he founded the Guardian Angels. He could have roped five shopping carts together and tried to clean Fordham Road all by himself. He could also have ridden the Mugger's Express and—like the taxi driver in Martin Scorsese's film or the solitary man named Bernhard Goetz who shot four muggers on a subway—Sliwa could have dispensed summary justice all by himself or with the help of a trusted companion. He had a history of being bullied, humiliated, set upon, laughed at, and shunned. He could have become a solitary avenger, a lonely little man who struck back after years of humiliation. That didn't happen. Instead Sliwa founded a group and appointed himself its leader. Its purpose was not just to protect the weak, but to provide a place for anyone, no matter who they were—black or white, Hispanic or even half Polish—to do good in the company of others. By founding the Guardian Angels, Sliwa found a safe place for himself in the world.

A Paralyzed Man

ED ROBERTS began by telling me exactly what he'd told thirty million TV viewers the night before: "I was a normal fourteen-year-old kid. A jock in training. Nothing special. I wanted to be a professional baseball player when I grew up. Then one night I went to sleep; the next morning when I woke up—bingo!" If Roberts could have, he would have snapped his fingers as he said this, but he could only move one of them, one finger, plus the head on his neck, and—he winked at me—his bladder and his bowels. Nothing else had moved since 1953. Fifty-three was the year Roberts caught polio. He and his whole family caught it, except they recovered and he didn't.

When they took him to the hospital, the doctors treated him like a dog who'd just been run over by a truck: they gave him plenty of painkillers and waited for him to die. When he didn't, they told his parents he'd be a vegetable. Thirty-five years later, Roberts has become an internationally known spokesman, advocate, and political organizer for the disabled. For fifteen years, every ramp for the handicapped built in this country, every parking space reserved, every grab bar in-   115 stalled, and every bus, train, and job made accessible for the disabled has been fought for and won by Roberts and others like him. Every year, Roberts gives dozens of speeches throughout North America, Europe, and Asia, and, if he can, he begins each speech with a joke about being a vegetable: "Here you see me, ladies and gentlemen," he says, "a living, breathing artichoke, prickly on the outside, but tenderhearted within."

He'd told that joke during his segment on *60 Minutes* the night before. During part of the broadcast, he'd been flat on his back in an iron lung, talking to a correspondent; during the rest of the segment, CBS had followed him to France, where he'd zoomed around in an electric wheelchair, sucking air through the mouthpiece of a portable respirator. As he was shown meeting with President Mitterrand and being greeted by the deputy director of the French Railways, a CBS correspondent recited his accolades: a recent recipient of a MacArthur Foundation "genius" award; the first disabled person to direct the California State Department of Rehabilitation; the first severely disabled person to graduate from the University of California, Berkeley; the co-founder of a breakthrough organization for the handicapped and the president of another—Roberts was a pathfinder, a trailblazer, a forward scout, the first of his kind to gain access to areas and activities that had never before accepted or accommodated people like him. What a black man like Bob Moses had been in the civil rights movement or a woman like Betty Friedan had been for the feminists, Ed Roberts was for the disabled. What made his activities so remarkable was that a bad cold could kill him and a curb could break his neck.

I'd known all this about Roberts when I'd made an appointment, months before the broadcast, to see him. What I hadn't anticipated was the effect thirteen minutes of prime-time exposure would have on him. What I also hadn't anticipated was the effect the very sight of him would have on me. As he spoke, half sitting, half reclining in his wheelchair, nothing but his head and face moved. He was dressed in a shirt and pants, but underneath the fabric it seemed that nothing had grown since he was fourteen. The result was the head of a swarthy, mustachioed, dark-eyed man, a man almost fifty, perched on the adolescent body of a boy; the man's head animated, the boy's body immobile; the man's head fleshy, the boy's body wasted, the two joined, but so disjunctive that, as Roberts grinned and his eyes sparkled while his body lay still, his head seemed to grow larger and his body smaller in my sight until, as he continued to speak, he seemed to become nothing but his head. His face, its variety of expressions, his eyes and their moods, his voice and its modulations, were his only means of communication, but these were regularly disrupted by his inability to breathe on his own. Like a Turk smoking a hookah, Roberts sipped air through the mouthpiece of his respirator. Sentences were punctuated by pauses, brief but distinct, as he drew air and the regulator responded to his demands. In ordinary conversation, people inhale and exhale and no one notices, but as Roberts spoke, his every breath was audible, as if he were a diver in an ocean of air. Now and then he shifted his mouthpiece, but since he could only use his tongue, his teeth, and his lips, his face became a grimace that had nothing to do with the meaning or emotion of his words. These sudden contortions startled me and, along with the misfit of his head and body, made me look at him as if I were an African seeing my first white man.

While I looked at him from a middle distance, Roberts spoke to me like an actor reading from a TelePrompTer. CBS had taped three hours of his life and times; everything he'd wanted to say about himself, he'd already said to the cameras. After an hour of me trying to fit his head to his body and him talking to me as if I were a mirror, we were interrupted by his secretary. We had been sitting in his office at the World Institute on Dis- 117 ability, a policy center he'd founded in Berkeley. Following his *60 Minutes* appearance, a meeting had been hastily scheduled between himself, his associate director, and the president of an ad agency that specialized in high-visibility media campaigns on behalf of such causes as clean air and family planning. With the help of a multimillion-dollar foundation grant, Roberts intended to present himself and his message, like Sarah Brady on behalf of gun control, in full-page ads targeted to opinion makers and CEOs who read *The Wall Street Journal* and *The New York Times*. I stood up to leave. "It's O.K.," Roberts said, and winked at me. "Stick around. You can be a fly on the wall." Two hours later, I realized I should have left when I had the chance. I should have left, not because Roberts, in conference, was boring, but because he displayed so little humility. Perhaps I'd expected an audience with Mother Teresa. I learned that was unrealistic.

For two hours, Roberts dropped names and boasted about his political connections. It was the summer of the '88 presidential campaign, so he spoke of meeting with "Jesse" and a personal call from "Mike" Dukakis. He revealed the backstage details of his *60 Minutes* experience: what the executive producer had asked him ("Anything you want to avoid?") and what he'd answered back ("Don't make me into Super Crip"); he called correspondents by their first names like old friends; his tense negotiations with the French Railways about handicapped access, he recounted like an eyeball-to-eyeball confrontation between the superpowers. After a suitable number of compliments from the adman and nods of approval from his associate director, Roberts switched to the purpose of the meeting.

The proposed ad campaign had a modest goal: convince health insurance companies to pay benefits directly to the disabled so they could hire and fire their own attendants. Between sips of air, Roberts summarized the argument: "Why pay a health-care agency twenty dollars so they can pay an attendant six dollars to care for a disabled person who then can't hire and fire his own help? Pay the disabled person six dollars, save the rest, and let the disabled person make his own decisions about who he wants to take care of him. Better yet, use the money to kill two birds with one stone: pay the six dollars directly to the disabled person and stipulate that he hire someone who's unemployed, someone unskilled but hardworking and honest who really needs the money." All that made perfect sense, but it was just a prelude to a far grander vision. "Listen," said Roberts, chewing his mouthpiece, "every democratic constituency you can name is fragmented, whites against blacks, blacks against Hispanics, Hispanics against Asians, women against men, gays against straights, young against old, one region against another—every single constituency except *us*. The disabled cut across racial lines, class lines, age lines, religious lines. What's happened to us can happen to anyone, and it will happen— sooner or later—to everyone. We're the only cohesive voting bloc left. We've all been tested. We've all survived adversity. The worst has already happened to us and we're still here. Mark my words, sooner or later, one of us is going to emerge as a leader on a national scale. Look at FDR. Hard times are coming. We're survivors and one of us is going to be there, ready, willing, and able to lead this country when things get rough. You know what the Marines say: 'When the going gets tough, the tough get going.' " The adman smiled. "You wouldn't have any ambitions yourself, would you, Ed?" Roberts laughed, and I began to look at him from a greater distance than before. As the adman talked of poster displays in bus shelters near the State Department and ghostwritten syndicated newspaper columns, I suddenly imagined Roberts, not as Edward V. Roberts, spokesman for the disabled, but as EVR, wartime President of the United States, rallying the people after a virus, engineered in Libya, had wiped out half the pop- 119 ulation, visiting hospitals, comforting survivors, his mouthpiece clasped between his teeth as jauntily as a cigarette holder.

All that would have to wait. It was late in the afternoon. The adman waved goodbye; the associate director returned to her office; Roberts told his secretary to call his driver. "Come on along," he said to me. "We'll go home, then I have to go shopping. You can meet my son. You know I have one, don't you?" I nodded. In the press kit his office had sent me, there were several pictures of him with the boy. As we waited for his driver, he spoke about his marriage. "Absolutely normal," he said. "She was my physical therapist. We fell in lust, then in love." He grinned. "Intercourse was normal. The birth was at home. Then we did what a lot of people do: we got divorced three years later." I was about to ask him more about all that when his driver arrived. The man had mild blue eyes set in a young face framed by a halo of white hair and a white beard. He and I went out to the van to lower its platform while Roberts finished up with his secretary. The driver was a Berkeley version of the kind of attendant Roberts wanted other disabled people to hire. Back in '80 he'd graduated from Cornell with a degree in English literature. His hair had turned white while he looked for teaching jobs. He was a soft-spoken man, glad to have work. Roberts wheeled out, rolled onto the van's lift; the driver locked Roberts' chair in place, then pushed buttons to raise the platform up and into the van. It was ten blocks to Roberts' house. The driver knew the route. Traffic was moderate and slow, but from the moment the driver pulled away from the curb until he drove up Roberts' driveway, Roberts browbeat him. "Stay in this lane," Roberts told him. "O.K., now switch lanes. Use your blinker. Use your blinker. Can't you hear me? All right, now turn your blinker off. You can speed up here. Watch the light, though. Can't you see it? Watch the light. Can't you see? Your windshield's so dirty. Don't your wipers work?

Use your wipers. Don't you have any fluid? Use some fluid." On and on, every fifteen seconds, Roberts issued a command or a complaint until the van arrived at his house and the driver, looking more sorrowful than after a job interview at an MLA convention, lowered Roberts to the ground, unlocked his chair, parked the van, and walked off to catch a bus home.

Roberts didn't seem to notice what he'd done. He wheeled up the ramp to his house. No one was home. "Grab that shopping bag for me," he said. After listening to him with his driver, I felt like saying, "No." "Come on," he said. "I have to buy some food for dinner." I walked beside him as he rolled several blocks, curb cuts at every corner, to a gourmet market. Roberts wheeled down the aisles like Lindbergh riding in triumph down Wall Street. A clerk at a fruit stand was the first to salute him. "Ed! Ed!" he called. "I saw ya on *60 Minutes* last night. You were great, man, great!" I followed, grocery bag in hand, as Roberts rode from stand to stand, nodding and winking and smiling, acknowledging the greetings, the calls, the hurrahs and huzzahs. He bought fresh apricots and spoke of tape formats. He bought salmon and told secrets about TV correspondents. "Here," he said to me. "Take out my wallet, will you. Pay them." Roberts waited as I completed the first transaction, then he swept ahead of me, deeper into the market, ordering items, acknowledging fans, leaving me to inspect his purchases, pay for them, carry them, and catch up. At first, I felt protective of him. I inspected what he'd bought to be sure he wasn't cheated. But as I fell farther and farther behind, as the transactions added up and the shopping bag grew heavier, I began to feel as if, without asking, Roberts had turned me into his valet. "Servant to a star," I thought. "A gentleman's gentleman." When I eventually caught up with Roberts, he asked to see his purchases. I showed him. "You sure that fish was fresh?" he asked. "Here's your change," I said. "Here's your receipts. Need anything else?" I'd never waited on a quadriplegic or a celebrity before. As I walked beside him back to his house, carrying his groceries, I thought, "Maybe he does risk his life for others, but I don't like him. His head's too big. He's nothing but an ego on wheels."

We agreed to meet the next day. I said goodbye and went for a walk. After a few miles of watching my feet move, I found a park bench and sat down. "You were pretty hard on him," I said to myself. "Just because he's paralyzed doesn't mean he's not allowed to be intolerable. Maybe you caught him on a bad day. What would you be like twenty-four hours after your appearance on prime time? Maybe it all evens out: he's accomplished many things against great odds. He's had to believe in himself or else, by now, he'd be dead. He told the producer at CBS he didn't want to be made into Super Crip. Don't expect him to be more than human. One part of him balances the other. Pay attention to the balances."

I knocked on his front door the next morning. Roberts must have known what he was doing when he invited me to his house. "Come around ten," he'd said. "I'll just be finished with my bath." "The emperor without clothes," I'd thought. "This is like the French court. Maybe he'll do me the honor of letting me hold his trousers." I stopped scoffing, though, when I walked in. He was laid out, naked, on his back, resting on fleece that had been draped over a steel shelf that slid out of his iron lung, a pale yellow cylinder, as big as an old steam boiler, that took up half his living room. A tall, lean, light-skinned black man was delicately dusting Roberts with talcum powder. Roberts turned his head to me. "Come in, come in," he said. "I'm not modest." He wasn't the ugliest man I'd ever seen, nor the most deformed, but the sight of him made me feel pity. He had no muscles below the neck. His stomach was a lolling sack of guts, framed by skin-and-bone legs and wasted arms joined to a pigeon chest dotted with tufts of black hair. His head was even bigger than it appeared to be when he was clothed. As I watched, his attendant slid a corset under him, centered his guts, and laced them up. Once he was girdled, his genitals became visible, a tiny penis nestled in a wreath of fine black pubic hair. Roberts had wanted me to see him as he was, and, as I did, I thought of the difference between Oz the Magnificent, Oz the Terrible, and the little old man who hid behind the Wizard's mask. Whatever Roberts appeared to be on television or projected to grocery clerks in public, he was a wreck of a human being who bragged for the same reason a man who could barely swim thrashed his arms.

Roberts spent his nights asleep in his iron lung. His days he spent propped up in his chair, sipping air and conducting business. As soon as he was strapped in place and his attendant had closed the door behind him, Roberts began telling me the story of his life. This time, he didn't speak as if he were reading a script, but he was such a public person who had told his story so often to so many that, more than once, his lines sounded like excerpts from a *Disabled Pilgrim's Progress.* "Here," he might have said, "was where I struggled for Control." "Here," he might have continued, "was where I Overcame Dependency." Again and again, he used words like "empowerment" and "reaffirmation" as if certain events in his life had become discussion topics for self-help groups. If I had been chronically ill or severely disabled, I might have heard and understood what he said exactly as he intended it, but, again and again, wrapped inside a story he meant to illustrate "Control," I saw "Passivity," and buried under a tale about "Mastery," I caught sight of "Loss." Nearly everything Roberts described as pointing upward also pointed down; everything he said pointed forward also pointed back, as if he were a teacher drawing a flow chart with double-headed arrows. Power and powerlessness, life and death, selfishness and compassion were at the center of his tales, sometimes hidden, sometimes not. How he came to actually understand and resolve these contradictions was the real story of his life.

He was the first-born of three boys, the older brother who did everything first, then taught the others. His father was a railway worker, a master mechanic and jack-of-all-trades who turned down every promotion he was offered because he never wanted to boss his buddies. Roberts' mother was a housewife, an intelligent and able woman who thought her place was in the home. The family never had much money, but, said Roberts, "we had each other." Polio changed all that. The Robertses went from being a family among families to being quarantined. It was two years before the Salk vaccine. The only defense against the disease was avoidance. It was as if a bomb had detonated in the Robertses' kitchen and instead of rushing to help them their neighbors ran away. After two weeks, the quarantine was lifted and Roberts was hospitalized with a fever of 105 degrees. In intense pain and delirium, he had his first "death dream." Over the next ten years, he had three others, each one spawned by a near-death experience, each one a chronicle of a death and rebirth. When Roberts was fourteen, he died and was reborn for the first time.

As he lay in bed, he dreamed he was fighting a war that wouldn't end. Roberts had always liked guns. Besides baseball, he loved target practice. At night, on the radio, he used to listen to news reports of the Korean War. In his fever dreams, he fought a war of his own, armed with grenades and machine guns, airplanes and artillery. What the special-duty nurse who sat next to him heard was a boy imitating gunshots and bomb blasts. What Roberts dreamed was an endless series of attacks and counterattacks against an enemy who refused to retreat. In the real world, Roberts could have been replaying the Korean War. In his dreams, it was

Death, not the Chinese, who kept on coming. At some point during a lull in the fighting, Roberts opened his eyes and the nurse ordered him to be quiet. Roberts shook his head "No" and went back to the battle. As Roberts now tells the story, his refusal to be quiet was his first political act. To say "No" to a callous nurse is now considered by the disabled to be equivalent to a black man refusing to bow and shuffle. Whatever the future political meaning of Roberts' refusal, when he awoke, he'd not only won the battle against Death but had driven the wicked nurse away. "It was my first triumph," he said. A triumph that left him alive but without a spinal cord.

The hospital moved him from its isolation ward to a ward of noninfectious "polios." For eight months, Roberts watched the other patients recover and leave, while the doctors waited for him to die. Finally, Roberts grew tired of their waiting: since he was almost dead already, why not be all dead and finish the job? Instead of fighting Death, why not collaborate? He decided to stop eating. A new battle began, this one between Roberts and the hospital staff. "Come on, Eddie," said the nurses, "open your mouth." Roberts refused. He wanted to control his life by ending it. The hospital wanted to control his life by sustaining it. Perhaps if Roberts were still healthy, he would have picked a fight with his father or his mother, his schoolteacher or his coach. Sick or well, able-bodied or not, he was still an adolescent in the process of defining himself by saying "No" to some people and "Yes" to others. His illness focused his struggles for independence and control on his mouth, the site of primal conflicts played out by every mother and child during infancy. The only things Roberts had left to move were his lips. The only choice he had left to make was to open or close them. The hospital said, "Open"; Roberts clamped his jaws shut. The hospital forced a tube between his teeth and fed him like a goose. They won and Roberts lost, but the entire process and its outcome were paradoxical: To keep him alive, the hospital rendered him more powerless than he was. To regain control of his life, Roberts tried to kill himself. The humiliation he suffered bred rage; his powerlessness increased his hunger for power; both states of being increased his need for control and made revenge a primary motive for any and all future actions.

Over the next few weeks, as the hospital force-fed him, it began to withdraw more and more of the special-duty nurses who had cared for him. Once again, the hospital and Roberts behaved in paradoxical ways: as the hospital rendered him more passive than ever, it simultaneously weaned him from the women who tended him. One day after the hospital withdrew the last of his special nurses, Roberts opened his mouth and agreed to be fed. As Roberts tells it, his decision to be fed was his second "triumph," a deed that marked his "reaffirmation of life." If that was so, it was also a triumph of the hospital: it had convinced him to open his jaws and take responsibility for his own survival. By depriving him of his freedom, the hospital had reminded him of how much his life was still worth.

As soon as he began to eat again, the hospital transferred him to its children's ward. Roberts became the boss of the place. Everyone else was younger than he was; most were there to have their tonsils removed. Roberts' age and illness gave him status. He was a permanent resident; they were tourists. He was an older brother; they were still kids. He ordered them about, sent them on errands, made them his messengers. He and the hospital janitors became friends. They gossiped; he listened. They told secrets; he kept them. The janitors were like country mailmen, bringing news from one farm to another, from one ward to the next. On the same floor as the children's ward was the neuropsychiatric unit. Harmless lunatics wandered in and paid Roberts a visit. He'd been in the hospital nearly a year. The world outside receded; the world inside took its place. Roberts became part of it. He was still in pain, though, pain that was best treated with massage. Again and again, he sent his messengers to fetch the nurse. At first she came when she was called, but then she ignored him. Roberts raged like a child who had nothing but anger to make his mother do his bidding. He needed to be comforted as much as he needed to be massaged, but the nurse spurned him. She wasn't on special duty; she had other patients and other responsibilities besides him. Loneliness, rage, pain, and dependency, the need for control and the need to be loved filled Roberts' heart. On the outside, he was nearly fifteen, but inside, he was still a child crying for his mother.

The hospital that had taken him in, nursed him, and stabilized him now transferred him to San Francisco Children's Hospital, a facility that specialized in the care of acute and chronically ill children. Roberts was placed in a ward with thirty other polios. In Roberts' version of *Pilgrim's Progress*, his transfer to that ward in that hospital represented his "First Sense of Community." He had gone from being a kid among other kids to being quarantined, then nearly dead, then "nothing but a vegetable." His age and illness might have made him the boss of a children's ward, but he remained alone there, too old, too sick, and too different from the others. At San Francisco Children's, he became a polio among polios. Misery loved company: he and the others had a wonderful time together. The struggles over feeding at his first hospital had left him underweight. San Francisco Children's fed him lamb chops, as many as he liked. He ate like a glutton and thrived. Once he was healthy, the hospital began to train him to live an independent life. After all his struggles for control, after all I had heard him say about Independence and Autonomy, I was surprised when he told me that he refused to cooperate.

The hospital's physical therapists wanted him to feed himself. Certainly he couldn't cut his own meat, but 127 surely, they said, he could raise it to his lips. "You like lamb chops, Eddie?" they said. "Then let's see you eat one." For Roberts, raising and lowering a fork was like pumping iron. After two hours of sweat and struggle, Roberts managed to eat half a chop. "That's it," he said. "I'm not doing this anymore." The physical therapists were upset. They knew what had happened at the other hospital. "Eddie," they said, "you're almost sixteen. Do you want to be a baby all your life?" Roberts' reply defined his future. "I've got a mind," he said. "I want to go back to school. I don't have a lot of energy. Either I use it to eat a lamb chop or I use it to study. I'm never going to get better lifting a fork, but I can read books. My body's no good, but my mind's O.K. Send me back to school."

The physical therapists reminded him of the obvious: he couldn't take his iron lung to class. He had to learn to breathe on his own. Roberts agreed. They taught him something called "frog breathing." As I watched, Roberts demonstrated. He spat out his mouthpiece, opened his mouth like a frog catching a fly, and took a gulp of air. He swallowed it and took another. The rim of fat under his chin stretched, then bulged. " 'Frog breathing,' " I thought. "He even looks like one. 'Ed Roberts, the Frog Prince.' " Roberts must have read my mind, because he performed his first magic of the day. One more gulp and swallow, then he said, "Pass me my mouthpiece, will you." It hung three inches from his lips. Whatever emotional distance I still kept from him I crossed when I handed him the tube. He closed his teeth around it and grinned at me. "Thanks," he said. "That was as good as a handshake," I thought. "Not as good as a hug, maybe. But a great way to break the ice. 'Hand me my oxygen, would you?' What a gambit."

The physical therapists taught Roberts how to breathe. They taught him how to sit in a wheelchair. For six months they worked with him. Then with one

A Paralyzed Man

day's notice, they sent him home. His family had changed as much as he had. First they'd been stigmatized, then they'd been deprived of hope: your son will live, they'd been told, but he'll never recover. In fact, said the doctors, he might die anytime. Chronic illness demanded constant care. Roberts sucked love and money out of his family. Frightened of him living and scared of him dying, his mother didn't sleep for the first two or three days he was home. Like the mother of a newborn terrified of crib death, she stayed awake, as if her breathing could sustain his. Roberts was as terrified as she was, not that he'd die, but that she would, or his father would, or they both would, and he'd be left, alone and untended, like a child abandoned on a doorstep. His first week at home was terrible, his second week barely tolerable. Then a tutor arrived. The family living room became Roberts' schoolroom and bedroom. After two weeks, he began to pass out during lessons. One morning, he woke up covered with acne. Day after day, he lost strength. It was his first health crisis associated with, if not caused by, schooling. It wouldn't be his last. He was hospitalized again, at a place called Fairmont. Blood tests revealed he was suffering from oxygen starvation. He had nearly no white cells, and a red cell count usually seen in people living on mountaintops in Peru. Frog breathing hadn't sustained him. Month after month of it, first at S.F. Children's, then at home, had nearly killed him. Every effort to make Roberts conventionally independent had failed: at age sixteen, he still couldn't eat or breathe on his own. His new doctors put him back in an iron lung. "At night, that's where you'll stay," they said. "During the day, frog-breathe on your own, but at night, let the iron lung do the work." For the first time in months, Roberts slept soundly. The dreams he had were deeply satisfying, but full of contradictions.

In his dreams, he was whole and healthy again. Somehow or other, a single muscle in his body had 129 escaped the polio and from that muscle others grew and grew until he could walk again. In every dream, he could walk. In one dream, he walked along the railway tracks near his home. As he walked past a house, he saw through the window a room with an iron lung and a wheelchair in it, but it wasn't his house and it wasn't his room. In another dream, he walked from one room to another, but as he walked, he noticed a wheelchair standing by a wall. In yet another dream, he walked again, and as he walked, he taught someone in a wheelchair to walk too. In every dream of recovery, there was evidence of chronic disease. In every dream of freedom, there were objects of dependency.

Once he recovered, he returned home. An iron lung now occupied the dining room. A special telephone was installed to link him to school. Funds from the California State Department of Rehabilitation paid for attendant care; money his parents saved bought him his own television. His mother devoted herself to him. His brothers envied him. A period of four years began in which he lived like a young monarch, waited on by an attendant, watched over by his mother, visited ceremonially, once a year, by his school class, as if he were a prince granting an audience. Every afternoon, women from the neighborhood, married women, his mother's friends, paid him visits. At first their visits were acts of Christian charity, marks of kindness, but then, like the janitors at his first hospital, they began to confide in him. Not just gossip about others, but secrets about themselves, hopes, fears, loves, and losses. Roberts, as he told me this, smiled. He had a friend, he said, as disabled as he was, a young man who had been cared for by nuns. The nuns confessed their secrets to him as if he were a priest or an ascetic—but he was neither. There was nothing he could do but listen; the nuns knew that and trusted him, his disability they considered a mark of grace, a badge of purity. What the nuns never realized, any more than the neighbor ladies who called on Roberts, was that even if a young man couldn't use his hands, his mind could still undress them.

His mother brought all this to an end one day. "It's time to go back to school," she said. Roberts agreed, but he was frightened, more frightened than he'd been when he was six and school was first grade. His mother loaded him into their station wagon and pulled up to his high school during lunch hour. A hundred students, girls and boys, all seniors, sat outside in the sun, eating and talking, flirting and fighting. A hundred pairs of eyes turned to watch as Roberts' mother unloaded his wheelchair, lifted him out, strapped him in, jerked him up over the curb, and wheeled him through the doors of the school. Roberts was nearly twenty. All he wanted to be was ordinary. All he hoped for was not to be noticed. Instead, a hundred pairs of eyes saw him. They watched him and reacted, without reflection or compunction, the way most healthy and able-bodied people spontaneously react to the sight of someone who's deformed or severely disabled: some were morbidly curious, some fascinated, some repelled; a few were amused; a few felt pity. Their collective gaze slammed into Roberts like a wave. He wanted to disappear; he wanted to die; he hated himself, his own body, his own deformity. Two days went by, two days of stares and whispers. On the third day, Roberts made a discovery: he was still alive. The stares hadn't killed him. His condition was no worse. He was still who he was. As soon as he realized this, he performed the first and most significant magic trick of his life. The ploy he'd used on me, the little trick with his mouthpiece, was just a bit of stage business, nothing but a card trick compared with what he did with the stares at his school.

What he did was transform them, water into wine, in his mind, from the stares of a crowd at a sideshow to the gaze of an audience at a play. Better to be visible than invisible, better to be present than absent, better to be alive than dead, was how the spell began. Wher-   131 ever he went, whatever he did, people watched. Instead of avoiding their notice, he began to solicit it. When he played to a crowd, its attention fed him. The crowd looked and its gaze engorged him. The crowd watched and he grew bigger and stronger. He practiced a mental alchemy: embarrassment became aggrandizement: people looked at him, not because he was ugly but because he was fascinating, not because he was repulsive but because he was remarkable. Disability became uniqueness, uniqueness became eminence. A prince with his own attendant; a young gentleman with his own equipment, he became the center of all attention. All eyes, all thoughts, all minds, he drew to himself; like a furnace, he consumed them. What he forged was people's acceptance, simple human acceptance. He changed "Oh! He's so weird!" to "My God, he's amazing!" to "He's really no different than you or me." That change in others' perceptions, from Ed the Freak to Ed the Miracle to Ed the Human Being, was the magic he performed every time he met someone new. It was a trick performed with almost no props on a stage nearly bare: feet that wouldn't move; hands that were frozen; all he had was his voice, his eyes, and his face, and, behind that, his mind, its guiles, its wiles, and its cunning, everything deployed to one end: to convince the world that he was a person, not a creature, a man, in fact, whose suffering justified sympathy and whose survival was worthy of admiration. First he convinced himself, then he convinced others. He practiced the trick on one class after another, thirty people at a time. The night before I met him, he'd performed it—flawlessly— in front of thirty million. No wonder he'd wheeled down the aisles of that grocery store like a champion in his glory.

When it came time to graduate from high school, Roberts' principal demurred: Ed was a fine young man, said the principal, an inspiration to everyone; he'd done better than anyone ever expected; in fact, he'd been an excellent student, but still and all, he hadn't met the requirements. The law was the law: without a driver ed. course and without a single, solitary phys. ed. credit, the young man couldn't graduate. What would people think, asked the principal, if we made an exception? In no time at all, everyone and his brother would be lining up, asking to be excused from the swimming test. Rules were rules. Ed had to be able to drive a car and swim two laps. The principal sounded like such a fool that when Roberts and his mother appealed to the School Superintendent, they assumed he'd solve the problem with a stroke of his pen. But it was 1959. Roberts was the first severely disabled student ever to attend his county's high school. The bureaucrats who administered the system considered it easier for a quadriplegic to learn to walk than for them to change the rules. Years later, when Roberts was working on his Ph.D. in political science at Berkeley, he studied the political organizing principles of the social activist Saul Alinsky. Alinsky had founded the grass-roots community-action Woodlawn Organization on Chicago's South Side. "A Big Win is what a young political movement needs," Alinsky had said. It didn't matter what the issue was, so long as it was obvious and the fight was winnable. A first win meant everything. Success bred success. Roberts and his mother didn't know that then. All they knew was that Ed was being cheated of something he'd earned. When the school board met, Roberts, his mother, and his father rolled up to the microphone, followed by a newspaper reporter and a photographer. The board knew they were coming. By unanimous vote, it waived the driving and swimming requirements for Roberts' graduation. It was Roberts' first fight, David and Goliath, against a public service bureaucracy, but it wasn't his last. When the next one came and the one after that, and the one after that, he remembered how he'd won his high school diploma.

A month after he graduated, Roberts' parents an- 133

nounced they were taking a vacation. It was their first
since Roberts was fourteen. In their absence, Roberts'
attendant would meet his needs. Roberts panicked: he'd
never been separated from his parents since his illness.
He was twenty-one, nearly twenty-two, but he felt as
bereft and angry as a child left with a babysitter for the
first time. Years before, when he'd come home from
San Francisco Children's Hospital, he'd been terrified
his parents would die and leave him like a foundling
on a doorstep. He and his mother had just cut their way
through a knot of public school officials, but that ex-
ercise in power meant nothing. The most emotionally
ill among the disabled bind their caretakers to them
with guilt. The caretaker becomes the disabled person's
mouth, eyes, hands, and mind even if the disabled person can, more or less, see, speak, or think for himself.
Each service gratuitously rendered weakens the recipient, and no service, no matter how lovingly or profes-
sionally provided, ever completely satisfies. The giving
famishes the craving. Needs breed discontent; discontent fuels rage; the disabled person becomes a black
hole that sucks time and life from his attendant. Roberts
was never as emotionally deformed as that, but, again
and again throughout his life, he suffered the pain and
rage of a child being weaned. To be safe *and* free, to
be protected *and* independent, to be enwrapped *and*
autonomous are contradictory needs that many able-
bodied people never resolve. Roberts' chronic disability
made him more vulnerable to the push and pull of these
powerful opposites. Child and man, he changed from
one to the other throughout his life.

Roberts enrolled at a junior college near his home.
He took a reduced course load, conserving his energy.
In spite of his caution, he suffered, early on, his second
education-related health crisis. He had great difficulty
urinating and felt agonizing pain in his groin. The doctors diagnosed kidney stones. When they opened him
134 up, they found a nest of them, one or two as big as golf

balls. To relieve his suffering before and after the operation they gave him morphine. As he drifted in and out of the pain and stupor, he had a series of out-of-body experiences. Roberts paused as he told me this. He took a sip of air, looked me in the eyes, and said, "They were profound; profound experiences." I nodded. In California, a nod is the appropriate response to such statements. Roberts described what happened: he rose out of his bed and floated up onto the ceiling, he said. I nodded again. I had read and been told of such responses to pain and morphine. Roberts continued: Sometimes he saw himself from above, looking down. Sometimes he saw himself from below, looking up. Once, while he was floating on the ceiling, he called in the nurse and told her what he saw out the window, accurately describing a scene he could never have glimpsed had he still been in bed. That sight, he said, was all the proof he needed that he'd actually left his body. Roberts looked at me and I nodded again. After that, he said, he kept changing his point of view, sometimes looking up at himself, sometimes looking down, until, all at once, while looking up, he realized that what he saw floating on the ceiling was his own soul. The sight of it made him understand that he had a choice: he could let himself float there and die, or he could call himself back and live. Roberts looked at me again, but I nearly forgot to nod, not because what he said was so clichéd, but because I suddenly understood how different such a familiar story was when told by a man who couldn't move, who, in fact, hadn't moved since he was a boy. It was one thing for someone near death who had never before been seriously ill to float up to the ceiling, look down, look up, and realize he could either float away and die or return to his body and live. Such a choice was easy and obvious. But Roberts had been making that choice since he fought the war with Death when he was fourteen. First, he'd fought Death and won; then, eight months later, he'd decided to surren-   135 der, but the hospital had forced him, then convinced him to stay alive. A few years after that, after oxygen starvation had sent him back to his iron lung, he'd had his first dreams of mobility, walking dreams, dreams of denial and acceptance, but dreams of movement. The only time Roberts could move was in his dreams. Dreams were his only freedom. His morphine dream of floating up and floating down, of choosing to stay or choosing to leave, was as real an experience of unencumbered grace as Roberts would ever have. Even if he'd been healthy, he could never have seen out the window of his hospital room. Sick or well, he was confined to a chair, a bed, or the sliding shelf of an iron lung. The choice he made, his decision to return, was remarkable because the body he returned to was as earthbound as a stone. Roberts was right: his hospital experiences had been profound. The dreams of a quadriplegic could be more real than his waking life. Better for him to live in his head than in his body.

Once he recovered, he returned to school. For the first time, he had an attendant he paid himself. The money came as always from the State Department of Rehabilitation, but this time it went directly to Roberts, not his parents. Before, if an attendant failed to please him, Roberts had to appeal to his mother, like a child complaining to one adult about another. Now, with the state's money in his pocket, Roberts became not just his attendant's equal but his employer. Under Roberts' direction, the attendant carried and wheeled him wherever he wanted, from the school parking lot to the student center, from the student center to class and back again. Roberts became a presence on the campus: he didn't just come into a room, he entered it with an entourage; he didn't just stop to have a cup of coffee, he deployed his equipment. In class, since he couldn't raise his hand, he called out his questions. Teachers remembered him not just because he was crippled, but because he was smart. The higher up the educational ladder he went, the more people paid attention to his mind and less to his body. He was a have-not who wanted to be a have; a dependent who wanted his independence. Power and powerlessness, control and obedience, will and passivity, these balances and imbalances he understood because he lived them. Political science became his major; the writings of Machiavelli, *The Prince* in particular, became his primary study. When it came time for him to graduate, he and his major professor agreed: the University of California at Berkeley was the place for him. It had the best political science department in the country. A bachelor's degree from there would be just the beginning. Roberts had the discipline, intelligence, and desire to earn a Ph.D.

The State Department of Rehabilitation disagreed. It had paid for Roberts' junior college like a rich uncle who knew he was indulging a child, but it considered a bachelor's degree, especially from a place as prestigious as Berkeley, a useless commodity. What would someone as disabled as Roberts do with such a gold-plated degree? A little knowledge was fine, but Roberts had to get a job. "Doing what?" Roberts asked. "Sorting buttons with my teeth?" Roberts' mother wrote letters. His college dean wrote letters. The Department of Rehabilitation agreed to an aptitude test. When the results came back, Roberts' case officer told him the bad news: according to the exam's personality profile, Roberts was both too aggressive and too dependent to succeed in a university setting. "What are you talking about?" Roberts said. "Either I'm one thing or the other. You've got me boxed in a Catch-22." Of course, the test results were correct, but the state's evaluation of them was wrong: Roberts' dependency bred his aggressiveness; that combination of opposites was a guarantee of success, not failure. Roberts, his mother, and his dean told their story to the local paper. A headline appeared: "Local Boy Denied Future." The accompanying story described how some heartless bureaucrats in Sacramento 137 refused to give a brilliant but crippled young man the college education he deserved. The paper ran stories like that for a few weeks, then the heartless bureaucrats in Sacramento caved in.

The admissions office at Berkeley remained to be convinced. The campus was built on hills. Not even the disabled veterans of the Korean War, enrolled under the GI Bill, had been able to overcome the terrain. In addition, there weren't any dormitory rooms big enough to accommodate Roberts, his iron lung, his wheelchair, and his attendant. The admissions office sent him to the campus infirmary for a medical evaluation. It was the best thing that could have happened. By coincidence, the Director of Student Health was a physician who had had extensive clinical experience in some of the more advanced treatment programs for polio. The sight of Roberts neither surprised nor upset him. He was an old and reasonable man. "Well," he said, looking at Roberts, "I see you've had a bit of a bout with polio. But you seem to be all right. And you say you want to enroll here as a student? Well, I know a good deal about people like you. There're quite a few of you, you know. You're the first I've seen here, but I venture to say you won't be the last. So let's see what we can work out." What they worked out enabled Roberts to enter Berkeley. The infirmary would become Roberts' dormitory. After all the doubts, quibbles, aptitude tests, and letter-writing campaigns, the solution was as simple as that. On December 5, 1962, the Berkeley student newspaper printed a picture of Roberts turning the pages of a textbook with a wand held between his teeth. Underneath, the caption read "Helpless Cripple Attends UC Classes Here in Wheelchair." Roberts was the first.

A month later, he nearly died. It was his worst education-related health crisis. Perhaps it was caused by overwork and anxiety. It began as a simple cold, but in a man as disabled as Roberts, no cold was simple. He developed a cough, then a temperature. He gasped for breath, but every breath was painful. His temperature became a fever; he coughed up blood; he felt as if he was suffocating. The infirmary diagnosed double pleurisy pneumonia. He began to hallucinate. Never in his life had he been so sure he'd die and never had he been so terrified of dying. He became afraid of sleep: if he slept, he'd forget to breathe. It was the same fear that had kept his mother awake for two days after he came home the first time from the hospital. His hallucinations became more florid and full-blown. For two days he stayed awake, then he had a vision: an old man came into his room. He looked like the director of the infirmary. He sat by Roberts' bed and put his head close to Roberts' pillow. He spoke calmly and reasonably. "Ed," he said. "You have to rest. If you keep fighting sleep, you'll die. Trust yourself. You won't die in your sleep. Only if you stay awake. All you're doing is killing yourself. Trust yourself and sleep. Otherwise you'll die." Ever since he'd been fourteen, Roberts had stayed alive by fighting Death. This time, the fight was killing him. "Get some rest," said the old man. "Don't fight it. Close your eyes. Go to sleep." Roberts did. He slept a deep and peaceful sleep, and when he woke up, he was no longer afraid. No longer afraid of dying in his sleep. No longer afraid of dying at all. For years and years, he'd been afraid of death. This time, his fear had nearly killed him. By trusting himself, he'd lived. He was like a kid who'd just discovered he could float. Simple facts like that sometimes change people's lives. Roberts' vision changed his. Not that his polio improved. He remained a chronically ill man. Fear never entirely left him, but it was balanced by hope. Death he accepted as a fact of life. He didn't have to fight it or surrender. He could just live. As soon as he recovered, he returned to classes.

He turned twenty-four during his second year at Berkeley. He still lived in the infirmary. One day, a nineteen-year-old girl was admitted, suffering from salmonella poisoning. The infirmary treated her with antibiotics, but she suddenly developed a blood clot in her leg. The clot broke loose, traveled to her lungs, and nearly killed her. During her convalescence, she spent all her time with Roberts. He was older and wiser, a man who had passed through many more dangers than she had. His humor comforted her. His optimism inspired her. They confided in each other. They confessed their fears and hopes. They became sexually intimate. Roberts fell in love. He fell in love because he discovered, for the first time in his life, he could care for someone besides himself. Up until then, he had demanded love from others. Taken their time, their attention, their devotion. Pleaded, wheedled, connived, cajoled, but always he had taken. Taken comfort but never given it. Never thought himself capable of it. Never thought he had any to spare. Again and again, he had been the needy one, the hungry one, the insatiable one. He had never imagined he could feed someone else. Or that in anyone else's eyes he was anything but a greedy cripple. The girl loved him. Loved his tenderness and empathy. His courage and endurance. His unselfishness. He had never thought himself unselfish. And, perhaps, until the last time he'd nearly died, he hadn't been. Chronic illness had made him selfish. Fear of death had made him selfish. Selfish, greedy, and antagonistic. A crippled narcissist. A sick man who always needed to be in control. Afraid he'd die if he weren't. Die in his sleep. Or die by an oversight. Fear had nearly killed him. Fighting Death had hastened his dying. That realization opened his heart. A year after he let himself sleep, he learned to love.

His change of heart coincided with his bachelor's degree. Berkeley's political science department accepted him in its master's program. In the fall of '64, he returned to campus just in time for the first student-power demonstrations that, by December, led to the unprecedented occupation of the school's administration building and the arrest of 800 protesters. Roberts went to mass meeting after mass meeting, parked at the edge of the crowd, and listened. As a student of power, he watched the struggle between the students and the university's president and board of regents like an ornithologist watching a mass migration. But he was more than an observer. He was a student of power because he was a would-be user of it. The Berkeley Free Speech Movement had been spawned by the civil rights struggle, and would, in turn, join with other political struggles: protests against the war in Vietnam; the hegemony of the U.S. military-industrial complex; the oppression of all minorities, blacks and Native Americans, women and homosexuals. A revolutionary leader-in-training, Roberts was in the right place at the right time. Black Panthers armed themselves and antiwar demonstrators marched while Roberts earned his master's degree. By the time Roberts began course work for his Ph.D., the feminist movement had formed its first caucuses and consciousness-raising groups on campus. To these groups, Roberts was admitted, out of courtesy, as a minister without portfolio, the ambassador of a passive, powerless, but angry minority allowed to listen to the plots and plans of another.

By 1969, there were twelve severely disabled people living in the campus infirmary along with Roberts. The Director of Student Health had been right: there were many more people like Roberts in the world, physically impaired but intellectually alert, some suffering from chronic illnesses, others from spinal cord accident injuries, but all eager for college educations. A technical innovation made their lives more satisfying: powerful electrically driven wheelchairs enabled them to go where they wanted, when they wanted, and by allowing them to dispense with attendants, gave them the privacy and spontaneity of movement that able-bodied people took for granted. To go out on dates without chaperons, to approach a group under their own power, to speak   141 with strangers and have the strangers address them rather than talk over their heads to their attendants— these simple freedoms exhilarated Roberts and his friends as if they were teenagers just old enough to drive. They organized themselves into a group called the Rolling Quads and in 1970 staged a palace revolt against the on-campus administrator appointed by the State Department of Rehabilitation to direct the benefit and service programs for disabled students. Like the inmates of the asylum in *One Flew Over the Cuckoo's Nest*, Roberts and the others rose up against Big Nurse, and with the help of headlines in the San Francisco *Chronicle* and the *Examiner*, demanded that they, the clients of the Department, have control over the programs that were meant to serve them. Once they were able to replace their foe with a friend, the Quads moved off campus and formed the Center for Independent Living, the first full-service support organization for disabled students. Twenty years later, that Center has become the model for hundreds of others established at universities all over the world. Higher education has become the great equalizer, the way disabled people can match wits with the able-bodied. Roberts nearly died trying to earn his Ph.D. The thousands of disabled people who have followed him are just as vulnerable as he was; without places like the Centers to help them, many more would fail than succeed.

From 1973 to 1975, Roberts served as director of the Berkeley Center; then, in 1975, Jerry Brown, newly elected governor of California, appointed Roberts to head the State Department of Rehabilitation. Revenge was sweet: a client had become the boss. For eight years, with a staff of 2,500 and an annual budget of $140 million, Roberts made sure that his administrators never paid more attention to the rules than to the people they served. It was from his vantage point as State Director of Rehabilitation that Roberts influenced federal legislation that gave the disabled the same access to opportunities and the same protection from discrimination as other minorities. Parking spaces for the handicapped and oversize bathroom stalls, physical therapy and mental health services, job counseling and employment training, all the medical, social, and economic services that might enable someone disabled to do more than "sort buttons with his teeth" were fought for by Roberts and his allies across the nation.

Every organization Roberts has founded or led, every reform he's instituted or pursued, everything he's done since he was twenty-four has been intended to help others avoid the pain he suffered. In this way, he resembles Sliwa, the Guardian Angel: suffering caused both men to invent ways to lessen suffering. First pain, then the alleviation of it. As a motive, cause followed by cure couldn't be more understandable. The Guardian Angels were created to protect people like Sliwa. The World Institute on Disability—Roberts' policy center in Berkeley—was founded to aid people like Roberts. The question remains: what kept Roberts alive long enough to do what he's done and what sustains him now? Revenge is one answer; so is the enjoyment of power, influence, and control; the ability to affect rather than be affected, to do rather than be done to. Augustine in his *Confessions* claims children are innocent, not because they lack the will to do harm, but because they lack the means. If Roberts could have, he would have picked up the nurse of the children's ward and dragged her by the neck to his bed; if he could have, he would have obliterated the hundred pairs of eyes that stared at him on his first day at school. If he could have, he would have. Instead, he devised ways to transform rage into will, self-loathing into self-love. Roberts' contradictions are many: childishness and manliness; passivity and aggression; dependency and autonomy; deformity and vanity. Like the cavities of a human heart, they expand and contract, pumping energy from one side of the moral equation to the other.

143

It is this flow, this transformation of forces, from negative to positive and back again, that sustained Roberts in his first years at Berkeley, and sustains him still. At the very center of his contradictions is the fear of death. His acceptance of death at the age of twenty-four allowed him to live his life in such a way that he could, for the first time, give himself to others. Fear of death would have killed him sooner or later, not just by preventing his rest, but by compressing him into a tighter and tighter fist that could never have opened. Giving and getting was what he learned when he fell in love, and giving and getting is what, on his best days, he practices. His contradictions remain, though. The struggle to resolve them is what sustains him. His imbalances keep him alive.

LIFERS

God's Instrument

ONE DAY Hollis Watkins' great-grandfather was crossing the corner of a white man's field. Hollis' great-grandfather was a singer, so, as he walked, he sang. The white man's dogs heard him singing and chased him up a tree.

Hollis wasn't supposed to have overheard this. At night, after the children were asleep, Hollis' parents and his aunts and uncles told stories to each other, secret stories children weren't supposed to know. Hollis had crept out of bed just in time to hear them tell about his father's grandfather and the white man's dogs.

The dogs circled the tree and barked until the white man came. He looked up and saw Hollis' great-grandfather. "Come down out of that tree, boy," the white man said. "No, sir," said Hollis' great-grandfather, a grown man with children of his own. "If I come down, those dogs'll bite me." "They won't bite you," said the white man. "Come on down." "No, sir," answered Hollis' great-grandfather. "I know they're gonna bite me." The dogs barked and bayed as he spoke. The white man lost his patience. "Didn't you hear me, nigger? I told you they won't bite you. Now come down out of that tree." "All right," said Hollis' great-grandfather, "but I mean to tell you—if those dogs do bite me, I'm gonna have to kill your dogs." The white man answered, "If you kill my dogs, I'm gonna have to kill you. Now get down." So Hollis' great-grandfather climbed down, and one of the dogs bit him in the leg. "Now get out of here," said the white man. Hollis' great-grandfather walked off with the dog bite on his leg.

Time passed. One day, Hollis' great-grandfather was crossing the corner of the field when the dogs came at him again. This time, though, he had a gun and he killed every one of the dogs. Time went by. Hollis' great-grandfather was riding in a wagon, taking a load of cotton to be ginned. Riding in the opposite direction, in his own wagon, came the white man who owned the dogs. As the wagons passed, the white man took out a gun and shot Hollis' great-grandfather in the leg, the same leg the dog had bitten. It took a long time for the wound to heal. Then, one night, Hollis' great-grandfather went to the white man's house. He crept up and looked through the windows. He saw the white man walking from room to room. Hollis' great-grandfather had his gun with him and—that's when Hollis sneezed. Hollis ran as fast as he could, but his father caught him and gave him the spanking of his life.

Hollis' parents kept such stories from him, as they had from all his brothers and sisters, not because they were ashamed, but because they were afraid: Mississippi was a dangerous place for black people to live. Young men and boys were rash. Too much knowledge too soon might get them killed. Hollis was nearly twenty before one of his older brothers told him how, long ago, their uncle Andy, a mixed-blood Choctaw, one of their mother's brothers, had hidden his family in an Indian cave, set a gun at every window of his house, and single-handedly held off a band of night riders who had come to run him off his land. Hollis was past twenty when his father admitted why he'd worked so hard to own his own farm: it wasn't just ambition, his father said, it was fear of killing someone. If he'd remained a tenant, his father said, he knew he'd get angrier and angrier, until, one day, he'd lose his temper and kill the white man who was his landlord. All this and more no one ever told Hollis until he himself had nearly died, two or three times over, fighting for civil rights during the struggles of the 1960s.

It's been almost thirty years since Hollis Watkins first risked his life by doing nothing more than sitting at a lunch counter. Thirty years, and still he conducts voter registration campaigns in a county where—even though blacks outnumber whites two to one—no black has ever been elected to office. Hollis is forty-seven now and gray at more than the edges; volunteers and voting-rights workers consider him a wise old dog, but even now, he still doesn't know what happened after his great-grand-father spied the white man through the windows.

The most powerful stories Hollis was allowed to hear when he was a boy were told in church. His grandfather was a minister in the Holiness Church, a church whose service was swept by ecstatic singing and speaking in tongues. It was in that church that Hollis' great-grand-father, the man who'd killed the dogs, had sung, and it was in that church that, from the age of four, Hollis sang as well. Hollis' father, the son of the Holiness minister, was a deacon in a different church, the African Methodist Episcopal, a denomination whose service was more decorous but just as devout. At the AME, Hollis sang in the choir, and after memorizing enough of the Bible, he became a junior deacon. One Sunday to the next, Hollis' family alternated churches, but whether Hollis sang at the AME or rose and rejoiced at the Holiness, he heard the same Bible stories, Old Testa-ment tales, stories of the Jews, told and retold as par-ables of hope and freedom. "God is not dumb," he heard. "God is not stupid. God is no fool. He *sees* our suffering. He *hears* our cries. He waits upon the ap-   149 pointed time. The time will come, and when it comes, we will be freed like the children of the Exodus." Years later, Hollis learned the secret of his mother's ancestry: the father of her father had been a Jew. For one forefather, Hollis had an ecstatic singer; for another, he had a man named Weiss. Together, they prepared him to hear the stories of his inheritance: Daniel thrown into the lion's den; Joseph cast into the pit; Moses drawn from the bulrushes; the children of Israel standing at the Red Sea; Joshua and the battle of Jericho; Gideon and his trumpet. These stories Hollis heard like a tuning fork hears music.

In his home, Hollis saw and heard other stories, parables of thrift, endurance, hard work, and success, enacted, day after day, by his parents. Every morning, long before everyone else was awake, Hollis' mother rose and made breakfast. Hollis was the youngest of her thirteen children. On mornings when Hollis' father and his two oldest sons were to travel to another farm to work for pay, picking someone else's cotton, Hollis' mother made two hundred biscuits, most for the men's breakfast, lunch, and dinner, the only food the men ate in the fields, the rest for the family's breakfast, eaten with oatmeal, sweetened with molasses, washed down with milk and coffee, supplemented now and then with jam doled out from one of the hundreds of jars Hollis' mother put up each season. Breakfast was eaten before dawn; work in the fields began at sunrise. Hollis' mother worked alongside everyone else until ten o'clock, when she returned to the house and made lunch. At noon the family came home and ate. Hollis' mother washed the dishes, cleaned the house, and then at two she went back to the fields, to work until sundown, when she returned to make dinner. She did this day after day, year after year, until all her sons had found wives and all her daughters had taken husbands, until there was no one left to feed but herself and the man she'd met in church when she was seventeen.

That man was a pure-blooded African, as black as any man could be in Mississippi. In his youth, he'd been a baseball player and a wrestler who'd competed in matches throughout the county. People said he was so fast, he could run alongside a rabbit and tickle its ribs to see if it was fat enough to eat. Even when he was middle-aged, he was so strong, he could pick up a wooden kitchen chair with his teeth and flip it backwards over his head. In 1948, when Hollis was seven, his father had bought 120 acres of land, planted cotton, and farmed it for the next thirty years, almost until the day he died. He'd begun as the tenant of a small landowner. "Lucky for him," said Hollis, because the landlord allowed him liberties that no big plantation owner would have permitted. Firewood, for instance: the landlord let him cut wood for his stove and his fireplace. Whether his father had to pay for it or not, Hollis didn't say, but year after year he cut more than he needed and year after year he sold it and saved the money. In the winters, he went to New Orleans to work on the docks and in the sugar mills to earn more money to buy his freedom. One winter, Hollis remembered, he came home with a suitcase. He carried it into the kitchen and set it on the table. His wife said, "Give it to me. I'll unpack it in the bedroom." "No, no," said Hollis' father. "I'll do it here. Call the children." When everyone had gathered, he opened it. Instead of clothes, it was full of bananas, bright and fragrant, fruit the children had seen but never tasted, part of a cargo he'd carried off the docks to earn his freedom.

The land he bought was thick with trees. He sawed them down and sold them. Red oak and blackjack oak he sold by the cord for stovewood and firewood. Sweet gum and pine, trimmed of their limbs, he sold as pulpwood; cut into board lengths, sawed by hand, the soft wood he sold as lumber. All the money he earned, he saved. Somewhere or other, perhaps in New Orleans, he'd learned how to make molasses. All around him, 151 anyone who didn't raise cotton planted sugarcane, but in all the district, two counties wide, around the town of McComb, Hollis' father was the only man who knew how to boil syrup. He sold his skill: the man who operated the cane press charged a toll: one quarter of the syrup produced was his. If a farmer's yield was eight gallons, the press owner took two, and Hollis' father took half of that. The family never bought molasses for its biscuits. Whatever they didn't eat, they sold or bartered, and whatever they earned, they saved.

All around them were modest farms like theirs, most owned by whites, but many by blacks. The Delta and its gigantic plantations, its feudal landlords and their sharecropper serfs, were north of them. During all of Hollis' boyhood, cotton ruled, and cotton was labor-intensive. The recurrent cycle of overproduction, price collapse, tenant evictions, and increased mechanization, a cycle further intensified by synthetic yarns like rayon, didn't begin again until the middle 1950s. Until then, those who could planted cotton and at every harvest they needed hands. In Hollis' district, those hands were hard to find: as soon as they were old enough, young black men took the train to Chicago or Cleveland, Detroit or Indianapolis. For longer than most, Hollis' family remained intact. When it was time to pick cotton, Hollis' father and his two oldest sons sold their labor. An average worker could pick 200 pounds of cotton in a day. A good worker could pick 300. Hollis' father could pick 500, and Hollis' two oldest brothers could pick 600 apiece. The family saved the money their sons earned. Even though they considered themselves no better off than most, Hollis' family was more secure than many. They had food; they had cash; they owned livestock and land; they had each other. Slowly, though, what happened to other families happened to them: one by one, as Hollis' brothers and sisters grew old enough, they left home. The boys left for Chicago; the girls married and moved away with their husbands. By the time

Hollis was fourteen, only he and his older brother Joe Louis were left to help their father. By then, the price of cotton had fallen so low, it cost a farmer more to plant than it earned.

Hollis began to work soon after he could walk. When he was two, he was given a gunnysack to trail behind his father as the man picked cotton. When Hollis was four, his family made him their water boy. Back and forth, a quarter mile from the house to the field, Hollis carried water to his family working in the sun. By the time he was seven, he was walking behind a mule that dragged a plow through the hard soil. He was just tall enough to reach up and hold the plow handles that framed him, level with his ears. His father had just begun to clear trees from the land. There were stumps everywhere and roots hidden just below the surface. The blade of the plow would snag on a root or hit a stone and the plow handles would jerk. When Hollis was older and taller, those jerks hit him in the ribs hard enough to break a bone or leave a bruise that lasted for weeks. By then, the soil was more cultivated and he was a stronger and wiser plowman, but when he was a little boy and those handles jerked, they slammed into his temples. Only good luck kept him from being concussed or killed.

As Hollis grew older and his brothers and sisters moved away, he had to work harder and harder. By the time he was ten, he could pick 300 pounds of cotton in a day. By the time he was fourteen and the fields had to be fertilized in the rain, it was Hollis who staggered down the rows, a hundred-pound sack of fertilizer balanced on each shoulder and a third one cradled in his arms. It was a matter of family pride that Hollis' mother had finished the sixth grade and Hollis' father the second, and that both could read and write and do sums well enough not to have been cheated by any white man. But when Hollis asked to go to school full-time, in season and out, Hollis' father nearly refused. Without the 153 farm, there was no life; what good was an education if the family starved? Corn and cotton had to be planted and picked; wood had to be cut; mules and chickens had to be fed; stalls and stables had to be cleaned. There was no end of work and fewer people to do it. Hollis rose before dawn to do farm chores before he left for school. When he returned in the afternoon, he worked in the fields and the barn until sunset. Darkness was his only excuse to study.

Hollis was eight when he first noticed the difference between the way white people treated blacks and the way they treated each other. His family was nearly self-sufficient; his brothers and sisters encompassed him; he never suspected his parents told secrets while he slept. One day, though, he went to town with his father. Few people had cash, and if they did, they preferred not to spend it on groceries. Instead, they bartered. The day Hollis went to town, his father carried eggs and molasses to trade at the store. Hollis' father had a list of things the family needed, ordinary things like lamp oil and wicks, sugar and salt. Hollis' father was able to barter for everything on the list except sugar. The man in the shop said he was out of it. Hollis and his father carried their packages outside and stood on the porch. Hollis' father began talking with a friend. Some white people walked past them into the store. Hollis' father continued his conversation. In a little while, the white people walked out. They were carrying sacks of sugar. Hollis interrupted his father. "Daddy, Daddy," he said, and pointed. "Look. They got sugar. The man must have found some. Come on, let's go in. We can get our sugar now. Let's hurry." Hollis' father looked at him; he didn't move and all he said was "Shush." Hollis wouldn't be quiet. He pulled at his father's sleeve. "Come on, Daddy. They got sugar. Come on, we got to go in and get us some." Without a word, Hollis' father picked him up with one hand, picked up their packages with the other, and walked back to the wagon. He unhitched the team and drove home. He never explained why he didn't go back in the store to get sugar. Hollis wondered about it for years. Why had the man said there was no sugar when there was? Why had his father not gone back in after the white people walked out? Why couldn't they get sugar and the white people could? Hollis was fourteen when he understood. "It was like I suddenly opened my eyes," he said.

What he saw when he looked around was a stone wall that was only a few feet from his face. Three things made him realize where he was. The first was the killing of a fourteen-year-old black boy named Emmett Till. Till was from Chicago, but he'd been visiting relatives in a little town in the Mississippi Delta. One evening, he made the mistake of saying "Bye, baby" to a married white woman while he was leaving a grocery store. Three days later, the woman's husband and a friend kidnapped the boy, drove him to the Tallahatchie River, tied the cord of a cotton gin fan around his neck, and shot him in the head. A few days later, the body floated to the surface. When the local sheriff shipped the corpse back to Chicago, Till's mother insisted that it be put on public view. *Jet* magazine printed a picture of it, gouged, smashed, and bloated. Thousands and thousands of black people all over the United States saw it and were horrified. Emmett Till wasn't the first black boy who'd been murdered for "acting smart," but the timing of his murder—one year after the Supreme Court's historic decision in *Brown* v. *Board of Education*—directed national attention to the way justice was practiced in Mississippi. The trial and acquittal of Emmett Till's killers mattered a great deal to black people everywhere, but it was the murder itself that mattered most to young Hollis Watkins. "He could have been me," Hollis said. "I was fourteen just like him. Those white people who killed him could have killed me. I hated them. I was afraid of them. I couldn't live with them. I had to get away from them. I had to do something, but I didn't know what."

The second thing that opened Hollis' eyes was a singing contest. Hollis was enrolled in a segregated version of the Future Farmers of America. The local chapter of that organization had an a cappella quartet. Hollis was its star. In local competitions, his group was voted good enough to compete against other singers from all over the state. Hollis' quartet won the semifinals, but the coach of one of the losing groups protested: he said Hollis' quartet had sung a gospel when they were supposed to sing a spiritual. People scratched their heads? Gospel? Spiritual? No one knew the difference. The judges deliberated and agreed: Hollis' quartet had sung the wrong kind of song. They were disqualified—disqualified by a technicality. Hollis and his friends rushed to their coach. The man listened and did nothing. "We felt cheated," said Hollis. "Legally cheated, and by our own people. That wasn't supposed to happen. Our coach made it worse. He wouldn't defend us. He wouldn't even appeal. He let us down."

When Hollis told me this story, I couldn't understand why it had affected him so deeply until he told me the last thing that made him see his surroundings: it was his father's refusal to plant anything but cotton. Hollis and his brother Joe Louis pleaded with their father: the work was too much for the three of them. They reasoned with him: the price of cotton was too low even to repay the cost of fertilizer. Finally Hollis argued with his father. By the time he was fourteen, Hollis said, he'd developed "one hell of a quick temper." He and Joe Louis used to fight all the time, and even though his older brother, true to his namesake, beat up Hollis every time, Hollis never backed down. His father may have been old, but he could still flip a chair over his head with his teeth. Whatever actually happened between him and Hollis, in the end the old man won. Hollis felt like a prisoner condemned to dig a hole and fill it again, over and over, day after day, the length of his sentence. His father wouldn't listen to reason; his coach wouldn't stand up for what was right. One man ignored him; the other let him be cheated. Hollis felt trapped: angry at his father; angry at his coach, he was surrounded by people who were even worse, people who were only waiting for an excuse to kill him.

Hollis had only two options: he could stay, hemmed in on one side, threatened by the other, or he could leave, like everyone else. Hollis had seen what happened to people who left: "They stopped being people," he said. To be a person was to know your neighbors and your neighbors' neighbors, to know their kin the way they knew yours, to help them the way they helped you. Once, Hollis had visited one of his brothers who'd moved to Chicago. He knew his brother's street address, but not his apartment number. All afternoon, Hollis knocked on doors, from the top floor to the bottom of his brother's building, asking if anyone knew his brother. "I'm Hollis Watkins," he'd say. "I'm looking for my brother Sam." "Never heard of him," people would answer through locked doors. Even the people who were his brother's next-door neighbors had never heard of him. Hollis gave up, went outside, and sat on the stoop. Sam came home after dark; by then, Hollis had never felt so lonely. City life dismayed him, but by the time Hollis was twenty and still living at home with his parents, the wall he'd seen when he was fourteen looked to be only inches from his face. In the spring of 1961, one of Hollis' sisters and her husband came home for a visit. The man worked for the post office in Los Angeles. Hollis' sister wanted to stay longer than her husband's vacation. "Drive back to LA with me," he said to Hollis. "Help me out. Keep me company. We'll get there and you can look around, see if you like it. If   157 you do, fine, you can stay with us. If not, you can go back home." Hollis had never been out West. He drove off with his brother-in-law.

In his sister's house in LA there was a television set. Back home in Mississippi, Hollis' family had a radio, but they listened only to baseball games and gospel music. No one listened to the news, no one had enough money to spend on newspapers, and no one but one or two white families in town owned a television set. Over the years, stories about the bus boycott in Montgomery and reports of Army paratroopers called out to protect black students in Little Rock had reached Hollis' part of Mississippi, but word of mouth couldn't compare with the sight and sound of television, especially when the evening news began to broadcast pictures of Freedom Riders beaten bloody and Greyhound buses bombed by white mobs. As spring became summer, Hollis grew more and more uneasy as he sat in his sister's living room and watched what was happening in Montgomery and Birmingham. Then, one evening, when Hollis turned on the TV, he heard a report about the Rev. Martin Luther King: Dr. King had declared he would accompany the Freedom Riders on the last leg of their journey from Montgomery, Alabama, to Jackson, Mississippi. Jackson was eighty miles north of the tiny town where Hollis was born. Eighty miles was no little distance, but it was still closer to where Hollis came from than LA. Hollis remembered standing up from his sister's couch and talking to himself. "What am I doing here?" he said. "Why should I stay? Why don't I go back home? If Martin Luther King's gonna come to Mississippi, I'll come too. If he's gonna come and do something, I'm gonna be there with him." Hollis decided to go back inside the wall. Maybe he thought he could jump out again anytime he liked. Or maybe all those Old Testament stories had had their effect: maybe he thought the wall would fall before he did.

158   A week after Hollis returned home, one of his friends

told him he'd heard a rumor: the Rev. Martin Luther King and "all those big people" were in McComb. "Where in McComb?" Hollis asked. "At the supermarket," his friend said. McComb was just down the road from Hollis' town, much, much closer than Jackson. The next day, Hollis and his friends went to McComb to meet Dr. King. No one at the supermarket had seen him. Someone said to go to the Masonic temple and ask at the office on the second floor. There, the only person they found didn't look like Dr. King. "Who are you?" asked Hollis. "Bob Moses," the man said. "We're looking for Dr. Martin Luther King," said Hollis. "Do you know where he is?" "I don't know exactly," said Moses, "but I can tell you he isn't in Mississippi. In fact," said Moses, "the only person here who's connected with Dr. King is me. I'm from the Student Nonviolent Coordinating Committee. I'm here to organize a voter registration drive. If you'd like to come in and sit down, I'll be glad to explain how you can help. That is, if you want to." Hollis and his friends weren't quite sure, but since they were there, they didn't mind sitting down to listen.

The first thing Moses did was pass out excerpts from the Mississippi state constitution. As soon as everyone had a copy, Moses began his class. "I'd like all of you to study these," he said. "Then, when you're done, I'm going to ask you some questions, because this is just the first part of what people have to know to register to vote." After half an hour, Moses said, "O.K. Now"— he began pointing—"I want you to take Section One; you take Section Two; you take Section Three; and I want each of you to interpret it for the rest of us. Tell us what you think it means. Put it in your own words. Because that's the second thing people need to do if they want to register." After everyone had had a turn, Moses said, "All right. That's fine. Next I'm going to hand out paper and pencil and I want each of you to write down your interpretations. This is what the regis-   159

trar expects people to do, and this is what we're going
to have to teach people to do. You can't teach a person
how to do something if you can't do it yourself." Another
half hour went by. Moses collected the answers. "Fine,"
he said. "That's it. If you would like to help, we would
like to have your help. But to do that, you'll have to
have your parents' permission. If they give it, then we
can get started." Hollis wasn't quite sure what he
wanted to do. The process reminded him of a high
school civics class, and Moses reminded him of a
teacher. Still, Hollis had come back from LA to do
something. He went home and asked his parents' permission. Teaching people the Mississippi constitution
seemed harmless enough to Hollis' father. The next day,
Hollis and his friend Curtis Hayes became the first local
volunteers in Moses' voter registration campaign. The
two passed out leaflets announcing night classes. In
three days, sixteen people enrolled, then went on to
register. Hollis was pleased by all this, but it wasn't
exactly what he'd had in mind for himself when he'd
seen burning buses and bloody Freedom Riders on his
sister's TV.

Farmers from the county west of McComb begged
Moses to begin voter registration classes there. In his
absence, a man named Marion Barry arrived in town.
Years later, Barry was to become the mayor of Washington, D.C.; when he came to McComb, he had already
been the chairman of SNCC. Unlike Moses, who believed in education, Barry preached direct action, nonviolent action, but deeds, not words, witness borne by
the body, not the mind. Hollis and his friends stopped
passing out leaflets and gathered around him. While
Barry told of the power unleashed by sit-ins begun a
year earlier in North Carolina, Moses was being followed and then arrested for accompanying people who
tried to register at the courthouse in the next county.
Ten days later Moses would suffer a brain concussion
after being beaten, in broad daylight, in front of that

same courthouse, by the county sheriff. There was
plenty of danger for everyone; Barry knew that as well
as Moses, but Hollis and his friends were so young, they
were afraid they might miss their share. Twenty of them
crowded into Barry's nonviolent direct-action seminar.
The first thing they learned was role playing: one person
was chosen to be "the nigger" while the rest acted like
outraged white customers. Everyone got a chance to
insult and be insulted, to abuse and be abused. After
the words came the blows: while "the whites" kicked
and punched him, "the nigger" rolled himself into a
ball, hands over the back of his neck, chin tucked to his
chest, knees drawn up to protect his genitals. One "nigger" after another learned how to roll around on the
floor like the dormouse in the croquet game at the end
of *Alice in Wonderland*. "Keep moving, keep moving!"
Barry would shout. "You stop and you're dead."

After three days of this, Barry told everyone to go
home and get ready for the real thing: the next day,
they'd sit in at Woolworth's. When the next day came,
only two people appeared at the office: Hollis and his
friend Curtis Hayes. "O.K.," said Barry. "If you got any
weapons, you got to put 'em on the table." Hollis liked
knives. He liked throwing them, blade first, into trees.
He could take out a hawkbill knife and open it, one-
handed, as fast as he could say his own name. At every
one of Barry's seminars, while Hollis was learning to
bear blows and turn the other cheek, he had a stiletto
in one pocket and his hawkbill in the other. He had
them with him, when Barry said, "Put 'em on the table."
Hollis did. "What am I gonna do?" Hollis thought. "If
they get me and start punching me, what am I gonna
do?" Hollis was strong. He'd been plowing fields and
picking cotton and chopping wood and lugging fertilizer
and fighting off his brother since he was a kid. Hollis
wasn't worried about getting hurt by anyone in any
drugstore. He was worried about fighting back. "If
someone hits me," he thought, "what'll I do? What if   161

I punch him out? Then what? I'm not turning myself into any ball. I'm not going down on the ground. If I go down, it's like surrendering. Then they can do anything they want. I won't let 'em. I'll run. That's what I'll do. I'll run."

"O.K.," said Barry. "Let's get in the car." He dropped them off three blocks from the store. "All right," he said, and nodded and drove away. Hollis and Curtis began their walk. Hollis felt delighted. In his mind, he saw how shocked the white people would be when he sat down and ordered a cup of coffee. He watched their faces, and as their jaws dropped and their mouths hung open, he smiled. He was going to rock their world. Turn it upside down. His smile grew into a grin. He was going to change everything. They were going to look at him and be amazed. He was so happy, he nearly laughed. Curtis and he kept walking. They passed the front of the store and looked through the window. "Oh my God!" Curtis said. There wasn't a single empty seat at the counter. Curtis was upset. "What are we gonna do, Hollis?" he said. They kept walking. "Think we oughta go back to the office?" Curtis said. "Maybe we oughta go back and ask Marion." They kept walking. Curtis kept talking. "Marion never told us about this. Maybe we oughta call it off." "No," said Hollis. "We're gonna walk around the block. We'll come back. There'll be plenty of empty seats. Let's keep walking."

When they came back and looked in again, no one had left the lunch counter. "Oh Lord," said Curtis. "I guess we'll have to go back now for sure. Don't you think, Hollis? We can't just keep walking around this block. We're gonna have to call it off." "No," said Hollis. "Let's walk around once more." When they came back again, they saw there was one empty seat. "What are we gonna do *now?*" said Curtis. "We're gonna go in and pretend we're shopping," said Hollis. "We'll go in and we'll wait." They walked up and down either side of an aisle of toys. Still no one left the counter.

162

They turned and began on a row of paper plates and party favors. Still no one moved. They were about to start on combs and costume jewelry when a mother and her daughter stood up. As soon as the woman had paid her check, Hollis and Curtis raced to the counter and hopped on the stools. The waitress who had been clearing plates at their end ran to the other. Two policemen walked up behind them. "All right," said one. "You boys better move on. You can't sit here." Hollis said, "Are you going to arrest us?" "If you continue to sit here we're gonna arrest you," said the policeman. "Well," said Hollis, "we just want to get served. We're gonna sit here till we get served." "All right," said the policeman, "then we're just gonna have to arrest you." It was as simple and peaceful as that. Ten miles to the west the sheriff of the next county had just smashed Bob Moses, face first, into the sidewalk. A month later, a farmer who had helped Moses try to register voters in that county would be shot to death by a state legislator in front of witnesses in the parking lot of a cotton gin. Back in McComb, the police did nothing to Hollis and Curtis except order them to walk in front as they escorted them to jail. "What are you charging us with?" asked Hollis. "We'll let you know when we get you inside," said one of the policemen. "Breach of the peace" earned Hollis and Curtis thirty-four days behind bars.

Neither of them had ever been arrested before, and for the first few days, they were frightened of being beaten or even killed. Their arrests coincided with Bob Moses' return from the next county with nine stitches in his head. The result of these events was an unprecedented mass rally at the Masonic temple. Two hundred black people came to hear a sermon of freedom preached by one of Dr. King's lieutenants who had come all the way from Jackson to address the crowd. Bob Moses spoke as well, but what was most unusual was Hollis' father: it was the first and last time the man ever   163 spoke in public, and it was the first and last time he ever declared, for everyone to hear, his support for his son. The day Hollis had been arrested, the only thing he'd told his parents was that he might not be home that night but that they shouldn't worry, since he'd be with other people. Hollis had never told his parents he was doing anything more than "working in the SNCC office." He had never told them about learning how to roll around on the floor like a croquet ball or about his plans to sit in at Woolworth's. After Hollis' father spoke to the crowd that night, people began to give him advice about his son. First came Hollis' relatives, the aunts and uncles who had told stories of resistance to each other after the children were in bed. "You better bail your boy out of jail or else he's gonna die there," they told Hollis' father. After them came white people who wanted to be "friendly." "You better talk to your son," they said. "If he keeps this up, something might happen to him." After them came black people who were family friends and neighbors. "That boy of yours is gonna get us all in trouble," they said. To all of them, Hollis' father answered, "That boy has a mind of his own. I've done the best I can to raise him. Now it's up to him. If he wants to sit down at Woolworth's and get himself arrested, that's his business. If it's all right with him, it's all right with me." That's all Hollis' father would say. He never went to another public meeting, and he never visited his son in jail. After thirty-four days, when Hollis was released, he came back home, but his father never asked and Hollis never told him about what he'd done or what he planned to do next. Their town was becoming a more and more dangerous place for black people to live. Hollis treated his parents the way they had treated him when he was a boy: "The less some people know, the better," he said. Ignorance protected them, but as Hollis took more and more risks, his silence and theirs made him feel more and more alone.

164   The sit-in at Woolworth's inspired others. A few days

after Hollis and Curtis went to jail, high school students sat in at the lunch counter of the local Greyhound station. Three of the students were arrested and imprisoned. A week after Hollis and Curtis were finally released, so were the students. When they tried to return to school their principal refused to admit them. This so angered the other students that a hundred of them walked out of class and went to the Masonic temple, where they offered SNCC their services. After much discussion, the students decided to march on the town hall. Accompanied by Bob Moses and other SNCC workers, including Hollis, the students stopped at the building's steps. One by one the students walked up to the front door, knelt, and prayed. One by one they were arrested until the police lost patience and did something never before done in Mississippi: they arrested the whole crowd. Nearly as soon as the students were booked, they were released in the custody of their parents, but everyone older than eighteen, Hollis and Bob Moses included, was held pending bail. Bail totaled $5,000, an unprecedented sum. Within a few days Harry Belafonte, the singer, loaned SNCC the money, but within a month Hollis and the others were back in jail, tried, convicted, and sentenced to thirty days for disturbing the peace. It was then that Hollis learned how to play chess and it was then that Hollis became a song leader.

Hollis had sung in church since he was four, but singing in jail was different. In jail, there was more to gain and more to lose: songs became weapons and songs became food. In jail, a song sustained its singers, then passed through the bars to strike their jailers. Singers changed themselves into the children of Israel and their captors into Pharaohs; songs turned them into Christian martyrs and their jailers into Roman soldiers. Morning began, not with a tin plate of grits and a cup of coffee, but the call and response, one cell to the next, of "I-woke-up this morning with my mind / My mind!   165

/ It was stay-ed on Free-ee-dom." At sundown, the day didn't end with a plate of rice and gravy, but, cell to cell, voice added to voice, "This little light of mi-ne / I'm gonna let it shi-ne / Oh-hh, this little light / A light of mine / I'm gonna let it / Let it! / Shine / This little light of mine / Lord! / I'm gonna let it shine / Let it shine / Let it shine / Let it shine." Again and again, stanzas repeated and verses added, the songs changed the time behind bars from tedium to fixed purpose, changed the place behind bars from a jail to a church, changed the people behind bars from prisoners to a congregation, changed despair to hope, dread to resolve, slavery to freedom. It was Hollis, with a tenor as sweet as an orphan's, who led the music. "Stop singing," the police would say. "Shut up!" the police would shout. Hollis would stop, but only for a moment, only to choose another song. "Ain't scared o' your jail," he'd begin again. " 'Cause I want my Freedom / Want my Free-dom / I want my Free-dom." Every cell would answer him, "Ain't scared o' your jail / 'Cause we want our Free-dom / Want our Free-dom / Now."

After his second arrest and release, Hollis never returned home. No one could hold his family responsible for his actions anymore. SNCC sent him west to Hattiesburg, then north, into the Delta, to Greenwood. Ten dollars per month was his salary, but he rarely received it. Instead he passed from house to house and family to family like a poor preacher riding a circuit. One place fed him breakfast; one place fed him lunch; the owner of a café gave him dinner. When he needed toothpaste or a pair of shoes, he mentioned it and, sooner or later, someone gave him what he needed or the money to buy it. Everywhere he went, he was followed by white men, day and night, on foot or by car. Often the cars had no license plates. Once, at night, he was traveling back to Greenwood. The SNCC office had been burned down two weeks before. He was driving an old car, traveling an unlit road. Headlights came up behind him. He accelerated. The lights came up faster. It was a pickup truck. The truck came close, then held a car length behind him. Hollis jammed the gas pedal to the floor. He reached 75, but that was all his engine had. The truck eased closer to him and, very gently, bumped him. It eased back, then closed again and gave him another bump. It fell back, then roared past him, cut a foot in front of him and slowed down, from 75 to 60, then 50, then 40, on down to 25. When it reached 15, Hollis pulled out and passed. He was up to 75 again when the pickup truck reached him, drew up, and nudged him. It did it once more, then it swerved out, only this time it didn't pass, but held even with him in the left lane. The two of them traveled side by side, alone in the night; Hollis' car stretched to its limit; the pickup cruising beside it with power to spare; the two of them gliding through the darkness like birds, wingtip to wingtip, except one was a hawk and the other a sparrow. Hollis looked ahead as far as he could see, searching for the gleam of oncoming traffic; he looked in his rearview mirror, hoping to see another car, any car, hoping for a witness. But, ahead and behind him, there were no lights; there was no one but Hollis and the pickup truck speeding down the empty road in the dark. Hollis looked to his left, and as he looked, the white man in the pickup waved. Then, as Hollis looked ahead and to the left again, the man turned on the dome light inside his cab. Hollis watched the man look at him and smile. Hollis glanced forward, then back. The man reached over, under his dashboard. He brought out a gun. He waved it in the air for Hollis to see. As Hollis watched, he leveled it at him. "He's gonna kill me," Hollis thought. Then he noticed that the window on the passenger side of the truck was rolled up. "He's not," thought Hollis. "He's not gonna shoot. He'd have rolled it down if he meant to kill me." And the man, as if he'd heard Hollis thinking, laughed and roared away into the night.

The people who wanted to kill Hollis preferred privacy. His best defense was not to hide but to stay in sight. Punctuality was essential: if he told a farmer he'd visit him at two o'clock, or if he told other SNCC workers he'd be back in the office by four, and if he wasn't, if he hadn't called, and if he was more than ten minutes late, people assumed the worst and spread the alarm. Once, he was arrested in a little town south of Greenwood. In the undeclared war fought in Mississippi during the sixties, jail was a relatively safe place to be: "accidents" happened there, but most sheriffs preferred people to die on the outside, beyond their jurisdiction, before arrest or after release. Besides punctuality, SNCC had a simple jail rule: when released, always call the office and ask for a ride; even if you have to wait, don't leave on your own. During the summer of 1964, in the town of Philadelphia, halfway across the state from Greenwood, a student volunteer named Goodman and two civil rights workers named Schwerner and Chaney made the mistake of leaving jail on their own and died for it. When the sheriff who'd arrested Hollis woke him up in the middle of the night and told him he could go, Hollis hesitated. "What did you say?" Hollis asked. "I said you can go. You can get out of here. Someone posted your bail." "Who was that?" asked Hollis. "One of your nigger friends," said the sheriff. "Now go. Get your black ass out of here." "Hold on," said Hollis. "I got to call someone. I got to call someone to come get me." The sheriff said, "You don't have to call anyone. You just go downtown there and stand on the corner long enough and some jughead'll give you a lift." "No, no, no," said Hollis. "I got to call someone to come get me." The sheriff began to laugh, then to curse. "You goddamn nigger," he said, and grabbed Hollis in an armlock and marched him to a window. "You just come here and take a look at this." He shoved Hollis' face to the glass. "Look," said the sheriff. Outside, in the alley, stood a deputy with two bloodhounds. "If you'd been stupid enough, we would have had those dogs on you

168

in a minute. See that tree over there? You would have been climbing that tree while those dogs tore you a new asshole." The sheriff eased his armlock and Hollis straightened up. He turned his head to the sheriff and said, "No, sir, I don't believe I would have run from those dogs. I don't believe so. If those dogs had come at me, I do believe I would have killed your dogs."

Hollis had been telling me his story for two days when he said that. We were sitting in the sun at a table by a window in a brand-new family restaurant in the parking lot of a shopping mall in Jackson, Mississippi. A beautiful young black waitress had just refilled our coffee cups for the fourth time. Hollis had only interrupted himself twice that morning, once to say hello to a black real estate agent and once to nod to the field representative of a black U.S. congressman. There were two white women and their children having breakfast on one side of us and a white businessman reading his *Wall Street Journal* on the other. Sheriffs, dogs, and murder seemed a long way off. Then Hollis said that last line. "Hollis," I said, "that's just about what your great-grandfather, the singer, said to that white man." Hollis paused and looked at me. He was wearing amber-tinted glasses; the eyes behind them were very mild; his voice was very mild. He was a finely featured man, slim and sinewy, his skin the color of our coffee. "Oh yes," he said, and smiled a shy smile. "That *is* right. That's what my great-grandfather *did* say. He did kill those dogs and I would have too. My daddy showed me how. You wait till they open their mouths to bite, then you put your thumbs in the corners and you take hold and you *break* 'em." He looked out the window. "I haven't had to do that for a while." He pushed back his chair and stretched. "Come on," he said. "Let's take a ride. I got to drive up to Lexington. There's an election there next month. Today's the last day to register. You can come along and we'll talk."

169

Lexington is the county seat of Holmes County, eighty miles north of Jackson. Hollis had been helping people register to vote there since the summer of 1964. Slowly but surely, in spite of threats, economic intimidation, and gerrymandering, the black majority of that county was beginning to win proportionate representation. It had taken twenty-five years. As we drove north, Hollis told me how the work had begun. In 1963, a black farmer named Hartman Turnbow called the SNCC office in Greenwood. He asked SNCC to send workers to Lexington to help people register to vote. Three out of every four people in Holmes County were black. If SNCC couldn't conduct a successful voter registration campaign in Holmes, it couldn't conduct one anywhere. A few days after Turnbow made his request, someone set fire to his house, with him, his wife, and his daughter in it. Turnbow's wife and daughter ran out the back door. No one shot at them, but when Turnbow came out, he ran into an ambush. The shots missed. Turnbow called the sheriff to investigate. The sheriff surveyed the scene, then arrested Turnbow for burning down his own house and shooting at himself. The SNCC workers from Greenwood arrived the next day. Hollis was one of them. The sheriff released Turnbow and charged Hollis and the others with arson and attempted murder. They spent four days in jail before the charges were dropped; then they rented a house and opened an office.

By the summer of 1964, Hollis had become SNCC's principal field representative in Holmes County. As such, he was given charge of twenty-two college students who'd come to Mississippi with hundreds of others to work for SNCC during what became known as the Mississippi Freedom Summer. Before any of the volunteers arrived, veteran SNCC workers had met to decide what to tell the newcomers about the state of the war in Mississippi. Hollis had insisted that SNCC tell the students, before they came, to be prepared for three things: to be jailed, to be beaten, and to be killed. The organizers of the Freedom Summer decided to delete Hollis' third item from the briefings the students received, but it was during that summer that Hollis himself came as close as he ever had to losing his life.

It happened, as such things often did, at night, during a car chase. Hollis had had as much practice driving the roads of Holmes County as he'd once had throwing the blade of a knife into a tree. When, one night, headlights came up behind him and stayed close, mile after mile, Hollis maintained his speed, biding his time until, just before an unmarked turnoff, he punched the accelerator and swerved onto a dirt road in the dark. The car behind him sped past before it could stop, jam into reverse, and follow. By then, Hollis was bouncing along a road he thought he knew, a shortcut that led past a farm to a county highway. About the same time the headlights showed up behind him again, Hollis noticed clumps of grass growing on the hump down the middle of the road. The grass worried him: the road he knew was too well traveled even for weeds. The headlights bounced closer to him. The grass spread to the tire tracks, then the tire tracks began to disappear in the grass. The car behind him was closer than ever. The road was turning into a path. Hollis grew very frightened: paths led into cow pastures and cow pastures had no exits. He was driving into a trap so distant and dark that no one would hear or see when he was caught. He kept driving, he had no choice, but as he drove, the grass began to fade and the road to reappear until the tracks became dirt, then gravel, then led, at last, to the two-lane blacktop Hollis had hoped for.

No one died that summer in Holmes County, not Hollis and not one of his volunteers. In August, all the students packed their bags and went back to college. One of them, a tall, lean kid with a stutter, named Mario Savio, shook Hollis' hand and made a little speech. "Thanks for everything," he said. "You taught me a lot. All I can tell you is: when I get back to Berkeley, I'm 171

gonna give 'em hell." Hollis thought Savio was just
being polite until, a few months later, he began to read
about something called the Free Speech Movement.
Savio had kept his word: he'd gone back to Berkeley
and helped lead a student revolt, the first in a series of
strikes against racism and the Vietnam War that, by
1967, had spread to every university in the country.

By '67, Hollis had left SNCC and been appointed
director of Head Start programs in Mississippi. Head
Start was a preschool education program funded by the
Department of Health, Education, and Welfare. As a
federal program, it became, in Mississippi, a place
where movement veterans like Hollis could find a salary. By that point in the story, Hollis and I had reached
Lexington and pulled into the parking lot of a ram-
shackle set of buildings and mobile homes that served
as offices and classrooms for a variety of political and
economic self-help programs. Hollis collected his mail
and his messages. It was Saturday. Anyone in the program who was working that day was up at the town
square chaperoning prospective voters as they registered
at the county courthouse. We walked through a maze
of makeshift corridors to a tattered conference room. It
was June in Mississippi and the air conditioning hadn't
been on since the day before. Hollis flicked on the overhead lights, then turned them off. We sat in the hot,
still room, and Hollis continued his story.

The Head Start job lasted until 1968, but then he was
fired. He never knew why; maybe it was because Nixon
won the White House. Hollis went out and got a real
estate license, but the market was flat, so he went into
the egg business. He'd buy hundreds of dozens of eggs
from hatcheries every Friday, load them into a van, and
sell them on Saturday and Sunday in black neighbor-
hoods in Jackson. Then, one week, all the chickens died,
the hatcheries shut down, and Hollis was out of the egg
business. That's when he became interested in raising
172   lambs. He knew pork was unhealthy and, besides, it

had been the food of slaves. Lamb, Hollis decided, was
the meat all black people would eat in the future, but
the future didn't come as quickly as Hollis imagined.
That's when Hollis went to work for the Black Muslims:
the Muslims owned farms in Mississippi, big ones that
covered thousands and thousands of acres. Hollis was
hired as manager of their farms. He lasted until the
Muslims installed a bright young Ag. school graduate
as his boss. The young man believed in organic farming,
so he ordered Hollis to use chicken shit to fertilize the
farms' corn and soybeans. Hollis tried to tell him what
would happen, but the young man wouldn't listen until
it rained and weeds, sprouted from the seeds in the
guano, choked out the farm crops. That's when Hollis
quit and took a job with a road-painting company. For
a year, he painted lines down the middle of highways
throughout the Midwest. As Hollis told me this, his
voice grew quieter and the room grew stuffier. Suddenly
he slapped his knees, stood up, and said, "Come on.
Let's check the square." From eggs to lambs to the
Muslims to yellow lines down highways, I was afraid to
ask what came next. The trip to the square saved me
the trouble. A long line of men and women stretched
around the corner of the courthouse. There were no
police cars and no pickup trucks. Just dozens and dozens
of black people waiting their turn to register as peace-
fully as if they were waiting to buy tickets for a movie.
Whatever Hollis did to earn a living, those people standing in line were his real work.

We drove out of the square and into the countryside.
We drove past farmhouses and mobile homes, past
barns and sheds, until we reached a red brick church
with a steeple. Hollis pulled off the road and slowly
circled the gravel parking lot. The place looked de-
serted. Hollis stopped and backed up so that the church
was behind him and the front of the car faced the road.
It was a defensive maneuver born of long habit. Hollis
turned off the engine and we sat for a while. Now and 173

then a car passed. Hollis said nothing and neither did
I.

Then I asked him a question I'd wanted to ask since
he'd told me about standing up and talking to himself
in his sister's living room in LA. "Hollis," I said, "did
you ever think you wouldn't make it? You said you were
frightened a couple of times, but how close did you
really come?" Hollis looked at me, then he looked at
the road. He smiled a little smile. "I was blessed," he
said. He shrugged as if he was embarrassed. "I was
blessed." He paused, then he went on. "I never came
close. Maybe once or twice I was scared, but—no—I
never came close. I don't know why. Maybe it was 'cause
of what I knew, 'cause I was careful. Maybe—but not
really. I think the Lord was keeping me. He was keeping
me alive to do what I could." He paused. "You know,"
he said. "We always used to hear in church, 'God is not
dumb. God is no fool,' and God isn't. God was using
me. I was His instrument. I was in His hands. In His
time, He'd see fit what to do with me, but until then, I
knew I didn't have to worry. He wasn't going to throw
me away. Any more than a carpenter would throw away
a hammer."

"You're talking like a man with a calling," I said. He
smiled at me again. "You know the story of Shadrach,
Meshach, and Abednego?" he asked. I nodded. "Not a
hair on their heads was harmed," he said, "because
God kept them safe. God calls people; God chooses
people." I led Hollis on. "Like the prophets?" I said.
"Yeah, like the prophets. He sent them out to remind
people they'd strayed. The prophets were there to lead
people back, the oppressed and the oppressors. Because
in God's eyes, we're all the same, no master, no slave,
everyone's a child."

"You're talking like a preacher, Hollis," I said. "Did
you ever want to be one?" Hollis smiled the biggest
smile I'd seen on his face. "Oh yeah," he said. "I often
thought of it, but it was too—confining. You're stuck in

174

one place with just one congregation." "So," I said, "you became a traveling minister? Is that it? A preacher with every black person in Mississippi in his congregation?" He shrugged, but he wasn't as embarrassed as before. "I guess you could say that was true. That was how it was." "But what about *now*, Hollis?" I said. "People are lining up to register. They're not afraid anymore. Times have changed. Why don't you just stop?" Hollis looked back at the road. A pickup truck passed. He didn't answer for a while. " 'Cause if I did," he said, "I know I'd die. It's not up to me. I got called. A lot of people died and I didn't. That wasn't my doing. So I got to keep this up until I'm not needed. And that'll be when I'm no longer here. When I'm no longer on this earth. Then I can stop. Then I won't have to do it anymore." He looked straight at me. "I was blessed," he said, and pointed at the center of his chest. "As long as I stay in the blessing, I'll live. The moment I leave it—I know—I'll be dead." "That doesn't make any sense, Hollis," I said. "Safety is jeopardy, and jeopardy is safety. It's upside down." "Yeah, it is," he said, "but that's the truth."

A Mother and Father

AUTISTIC CHILDREN first appeared in fairy tales as beautiful babies stolen by fairies who wanted them for their own. In their place, the fairies left pieces of wood carved to look like the stolen children and endowed by magic with the semblance of life. Alien and aloof, the replicas acted alive but were inert, appeared human but weren't.

For centuries, autistic children inhabited only the literature of make-believe. Then, ten years after the French Revolution, an abandoned boy was found wandering in a forest in southern France. The boy acted so strangely that people said he had been raised by wolves. Since he couldn't talk and acted as if he couldn't hear, he was put in the care of a physician who had founded an institution for deaf-mutes. The boy was given the name of Victor. His doctor kept a journal of his efforts to teach the boy to speak and act in a civilized fashion; thus Victor became the first autistic child to enter medical literature. Even though he never looked at people or played with toys, Victor displayed a remarkable visual memory: if something in his room was moved even slightly, he became terribly upset until it was restored to its exact place. Victor's hearing was just as paradoxical: the sudden noise of a pistol shot didn't startle him, but if a walnut was cracked in the next room, he came running to beg for a tidbit.

In 1919, the director of an insane asylum in Zurich coined the term "autistic" to describe adult schizophrenics who had sunk into themselves. Nearly thirty years went by. Then an American psychologist named Leo Kanner used the term again, but this time to describe the symptoms of nearly a hundred children, all of whom had withdrawn from human contact. Some of the children were mute; some repeated words like echoes. Any of them could have been Victor, except none had been abandoned in a forest: all were the attractive children of unusually intelligent, well-to-do parents. Because of the children's social and economic origins, autism soon became known as a childhood pathology of the professional classes: not the avarice of fairies, but the coldness of overeducated mothers and the self-absorption of overly ambitious fathers turned flesh and blood into wooden statues. Today, autism is thought to be the manifestation of an organic brain disorder—not the result of poor parenting, but a defect in the cerebellum, the hippocampus, and the left temporal hemisphere. Still, the exact causes of the disease are not known. Autism remains an illness without a cure, a psychosis defined by its behaviors. Four times more boys than girls suffer from it. Most autistic children are retarded; 60 percent have IQs below 50. In the general population, autism occurs more often than congenital blindness, just as often as congenital deafness, but it is a disease far more devastating to a child's parents than the failure of a single sense organ.

Some of the more famous accounts of the all-encompassing nature of the illness, written over the past thirty years by parents and psychiatrists, have had the word "siege" or "fortress" in their titles. And for good reason: trying to communicate with an autistic child is equiv- 177 alent to tapping a coded message through a stone wall to a prisoner shut in a cell. The child looks out at the world and the people who love him through ordinary eyes, set in a pleasant face, carried about by a normal body, but the child gives little evidence of sensing what is signaled. Again and again, the parents tap the same simple message against the wall. Sometimes the child laughs, sometimes the child cries, just as often he screams, but rarely does he answer. Laughter and tears reveal the presence of a soul; a face and body that resemble the parents' give evidence of the child's humanity, but year after year, the mother and the father tap the same message against the stone, and year after year, they wait for a reply. If their lives were fables, they would die at their posts, still waiting for an answer. In fact, many give up long before they grow old. Many leave each other; sometimes they divorce; sometimes they desert. Occasionally, they remain together, but use such distractions as alcohol or jobs to deaden the rage, grief, and guilt they feel. Most often, they place the child in an institution and visit him once in a while. Sometimes, they don't visit him at all. Few continue to tap their messages against the wall of his cell. And few, very few, live lives without sorrow.

What follows is the story of a mother and a father who neither abandoned their son in the forests of an asylum nor left each other. Unlike the parents of the children that Kanner, the American psychologist, first studied, neither of these parents is a professional or well educated: Carl Smith's present job is cleaning toilets in a General Motors plant; he's worked there for twenty-seven years. The best job Jane Smith has ever had, a job she's done for ten years, is standing at the cash register of a Burger King and asking, "May I take your order, please?" Keith, their son, is twenty years old. He's a handsome young man, with thick dark hair, bright blue eyes, and a finely formed mouth. Depending on the test he takes, he has a mental age of either three years eight months or five years two months. His IQ is no lower than 38 and no higher than 47. He lives at home; he goes to school. Carl and Jane could have institutionalized him long ago. Their second child, two years younger than Keith, is an active, pretty girl of above-average intelligence. Carl and Jane could have committed Keith to a residential center and devoted themselves to their daughter. Instead, they kept Keith in the family.

Seen from the outside, nothing about the Smiths—certainly not their name—appears remarkable: they live in a fifties ranch-style house at the end of a cul-de-sac bulldozed from a grove of pines fifteen miles west of the towers and office buildings of Atlanta. Jane has the face and grooming of a grade-school teacher or a phone company service manager. Carl is more thickset, not stumpy but solid, with dark eyes, a broad nose, and high cheekbones inherited from a Cherokee great-grandmother. Both Carl and Jane come from country families. Carl, especially, still speaks in a country way, using sentences like "She learned him to tie his shoes." But Carl's grammar, Jane's job, and the place they live have nothing to do with the nature of their hearts. It was their hearts that enabled them to care for Keith, but it was their hearts they risked to do what they did. What follow are the stories of two lives as common but as uncommon as passages from a parable.

Carl dropped out of school and left home when he was sixteen. He wandered around for the next eight years until his first cousin introduced him to Jane. Carl is a literal-minded man. If he were still a farmer like some of his ancestors, he might have recalled his past in terms of the crops he'd planted or the livestock he'd bought and sold. Instead, he remembered his years of living on his own by recalling the cars he'd owned, reciting year, make, and model like a man telling beads.

First was a '54 Pontiac. Not new, but good enough 179

to get him out of the house and back and forth to Texas a few times. Back and forth to whose house, where, and how many times, Carl never exactly explained. He spoke to me with an effort. He tried to be precise, tried to recall time, place, and date, tried to use just the right words, but he tried too hard. His speech changed from ponderous to delicate then back again; his sentences lumbered around like cartoon elephants in tutus. Out of Carl's mouth would come "That sure was a good car." Then he'd look at me and correct himself. "Ve-hi-cle," he'd say. "That sure was a good ve-hi-cle." He knew he was talking to an author. Someone who'd put him in a book. Someone who noticed what he said. Words made him nervous. So nervous that, in the beginning, I kept quiet and let him tell his story however he was able. At first, like an elephant in the cartoon, he'd look at his feet and stumble, but, over time, he forgot I was anyone special, and his words came out free, colloquial, and graceful. The longer he talked, the less he stumbled and the more questions I could ask him.

The '54 Pontiac was how he began. Back and forth between somewhere in Texas and Warren, Ohio, which is where his father worked for Republic Steel for thirty-five years. Or back and forth between somewhere in Texas and his family's homeplace, which was and always had been in a little Georgia mountain town called Blairsville, just across the state line from Murphy, North Carolina, which was where Jane's family lived, mother's side and father's side, seventeen brothers and two sisters in all, and every single one of them settled within three or four miles of each other.

In Texas, Carl worked as a carpenter's helper, then as a roofer—grunt work, but all he could get. He came back home and left several times. For two years, he even lived in Cleveland, Ohio, where he learned how to operate a metal-cutting lathe in a gear shop. Finally, he left home for good. "Home" may have been Blairs-

couple more stories like that, all of them just as crude and just as funny, their humor based on someone's impertinence and someone else's stupidity. Carl laughed at every story and I laughed with him. Then he paused. "Keith," he said, "he laughs at the same things. His favorite's the Three Stooges. He gets the biggest kick out of those fellas. He can sit and laugh at them all day. He must have inherited his sense of humor, don't you think? You think people do that?" I said I didn't know.

Carl nodded and went back to talking about his grandparents. He loved them, he said, but he thought they were slow. "How do you mean?" I asked. Carl explained: His job was to set the table for dinner. He'd been taught to turn the plates face down because of the flies. One night, his grandparents and his uncle came home and sat down at the table. They'd been working all day and they were tired. His grandmother dished out the food and the three of them ate it off the bottoms of their plates. They didn't even notice. A few days later, Carl decided to play a joke on them: His grandmother wasn't a very good housekeeper. She often didn't wash the breakfast dishes. Carl took them out of the sink one afternoon and set them on the ~~... same~~ thing happened that night as before: the thr~~...~~ home from work, his grandmother dished o~~...~~ and they all ate it, no more noticing when their p~~...~~ were dirty than they had when they were upside down. "That's what I call slow," said Carl.

Carl was neither as dumb nor as coarse as his relatives, but when I asked him about his schooling, I began to understand that Keith may have inherited more than his sense of humor. Carl was embarrassed by my asking about school, but he answered me. He repeated first grade, he said. At least he thought so. He was pretty sure. And, he thought, he'd repeated fifth grade. Or maybe it was sixth. He wasn't sure. He remembered he repeated one of them, but just once. Then, when he was sixteen, he dropped out. He was doing ninth- or tenth-

ville by then, since he spoke of driving down to Atlanta. What he drove was the most glamorous car he'd ever own: a 1958 pink Catalina convertible. Roof down, hair blowing in the wind, he entered the capital of the New South. To use his words, he "took up residence" in rooming houses. All he had was a suitcase, so when the rent came due, he left. Or, as he said, he "va-cated." In two months, he lived in fourteen places. Then he applied for a job with General Motors. Northern corporations have always loved the South for its nonunion wages. The labor of two people like Carl—unskilled, without even a high school diploma—could be purchased in Georgia for what one man would cost north of the Ohio River. But in Cleveland, Carl had joined the UAW. For someone like him, union wages in an automobile plant were the best he could ever hope for.

In the early sixties, GM operated two plants in Atlanta, one near the federal penitentiary, just south of downtown, that produced a blue whale of a Chevrolet called the Caprice, and another plant, north and east of the city, a huge operation that pumped out a variety of showboat Buicks, Oldsmobiles, and Pontiacs. The northside plant called Carl first. By then, his pink Catalina had been totaled, broadsided by a carload of drunks one weekend when Carl was on a date up in the mountains. To get to work, he bought a "junker," a rusted-out '55 Plymouth from up North that had just enough left in it to get him in and out of the company parking lot. GM put him on the first shift on a main assembly line. The work was so hard, he wondered if he'd break down before the Plymouth. He lasted longer than the car. GM transferred him to the second shift and a different job. He felt so relieved, he went out and bought himself a "rocket," a '53 Ford coupe with a 427-cubic-inch engine, a four-barrel carburetor, and a positraction rear end. Unfortunately, it was a lemon. He drove it until someone stole it from behind his boardinghouse, stripped it, and set it on fire in some woods.

He used the insurance to buy a '65 Olds. It was his first new car, bought from a dealer. It was also his second lemon, but it looked good. It was what he was driving when he met Jane. At the time, she was behind the wheel of a '57 Chevy. "A real sharp car," Carl said.

Carl would have continued listing the cars of his life if I hadn't interrupted him to ask about his parents. It was my first direct question and it worried him. He stopped and thought. I didn't know it then, but I should have asked instead about his grandparents. Still, he tried to oblige. He was born, he said, in 1941, and nearly as soon as he could breathe, his father moved the whole family north to Ohio. For two years, Carl's father worked in the steel mills, then he was drafted. Carl's mother took the family back to Georgia to live with her parents. Georgia was where Carl's memories began. The first was being held up to a window to see his great-grandmother, the Cherokee, laid out in her coffin, dead at the age of 104. The second was standing and watching his father come riding home on the back of a mule, back from the war, back from the Pacific. "What did he do there?" I asked. "He buried people," Carl said, Americans and Japanese. Carl's father had been a gravedigger. As soon as he could, he moved the family North again, back to Ohio. For the rest of his life, he operated a crane. Carl stopped there, as if he'd come to a blank spot. "And your mother?" I prompted. "She worked for the Ravenna Arsenal," Carl said, "then Packard Electric. She did it seventeen years, then she hurt her back and had to quit. She started using a lot of those painkillers, but nobody paid attention to her. That's what killed her." Carl stopped again, as if he'd come to another blank spot. "How did you feel about her?" I asked. Carl looked startled. "Oh," he said, "she was always there for me. Yes, sir, she was always there when I needed her." He stopped again and waited. That's when I thought to ask about his grandparents. It

was the right question. He started talking a while, he didn't stop.

The mountains of northern Georgia, along t with North Carolina and Tennessee, are hea ested. Whatever Carl's grandfather did before born, he ran a sawmill when Carl knew him. a big mill, just a shed with a diesel engine co to a wide belt that turned a big circular saw an a flatbed carriage that moved logs into the saw Carl's favorite story about his grandfather ha with the saw belt and Carl's uncle Ronald: it wa ting time and his grandfather had shut off the The belt kept turning, though. Carl's grandfathe at one end of the shed, by the engine; Uncle R stood at the other, by the far end of the belt. Carl's words: His uncle took out his pecker and on the belt. The belt carried the piss down to grandfather. As the belt turned, it splashed the p the air and showered it on the old man. The old didn't know that, though. Instead, he stuck out his to see if it was raining. He realized it wasn't whe looked down at Ronald and saw him shaking the drop off his pecker and laughing. The old man cha Ronald a half mile, all the way back to the house.

Carl laughed when he told me this. I did too, so told me another. His grandmother, he said, played most the same trick on him. "Where does milk cor from?" Carl asked her one day. He must have been ve young. "Come on down to the barn and I'll show you said his grandmother. They walked over to the fami cow. His grandmother sat down on a stool. "Ben down," she said to Carl. Carl bent. "Lower," she said He bent some more. "No, lower," she said, until hi face was even with the cow's udder. Then she grabbed a tit and squirted Carl in the eye. She laughed and laughed, and every time she thought about it for the rest of the day, she laughed some more. Carl told a

grade work, he couldn't remember exactly. Carl looked as if he were in pain as he said this. He just wasn't good at schoolwork, he said. He was a good runner, though. A real good runner. In English he did pretty well. Math was his worst. That hurt his pride. It hurt him inside. He thought to himself, "Why stay around a place if everything makes you feel no good?" So he left. He left school and he left home, and he began to wander. When he turned eighteen, he tried to get into the Army. They turned him down. Thirty years later, as he told me this, he sounded mortified. "Yeah, Mike," he said, "they turned me down. I tried the Marines too, and they turned me down." It was hard to bear. There hadn't been anything physically wrong with him, no flat feet, no hernias. He just couldn't pass the written tests. Back in 1959, people would have called him stupid, but Carl wasn't and isn't stupid. Today, he'd be classified as learning-disabled: a person of average intelligence whose performance was less than his intellectual capacity. *That* was something Keith was likely to have inherited.

General Motors put Carl to work bolting control arms to frames as they passed on the line. Control arms connect the stem of each wheel to an automobile's frame. Three bolts hold each arm in place. Installing them is a simple procedure but "it damn near killed me," Carl said. After a week of it, an assistant manager came roaring down from his office and backed Carl's foreman against the wall. The man in the white shirt was so mad, everyone could hear him above the noise. "Get those bozos off the line," he shouted. Whatever Carl and another new worker had been doing, they'd done it so badly that the number of rejects and repairs had violated even the quality-control standards GM used in the sixties. "Fire 'em," the manager yelled, and left. As soon as the man was gone, Carl's foreman pulled him off the line. Carl had tried hard but he'd failed. His foreman took pity on him: he gave him another chance on the 185

second shift. Carl did subassembly there: he put together power-steering units; then he worked on bump-
ers. Then he got lucky: he became a driver. As finished
cars came off the line, their windshields had grease-
pencil marks on them, made by inspectors, indicating
what, if any, repairs were needed: air conditioning or
paint, steering or suspension, engine or transmission.
Drivers stood in line, ready to take the cars where they
needed to go. "It sounds easy," said Carl, "but that's a
big plant. There was a lot of walking involved." Carl
did it for fourteen years. Back in '83, they switched him
to maintenance.

"So how'd you meet Jane?" I asked. Carl smiled. It
was another good question. "One of my cousins," he
said. "She introduced us. She used to double-date with
Jane." They met in June and were married in November. They lived in apartments in Atlanta for a few years;
Carl worked his shift at GM; Jane worked a different
schedule somewhere else; weekends were their times
together. Then, in 1969, Jane got pregnant, and in June,
one week after Carl's birthday, she gave birth to Keith.
Carl said that Jane knew from the beginning that something was wrong with Keith, but Carl didn't know or
wouldn't believe it until the boy was five.

When Keith was a baby, he never slept and he never
reached out. He screamed all the time. "You mean he
cried?" I asked. "No," said Carl. "He screamed." He
was always sick with a cold or an ear infection. Since
he screamed so much, they always feared the worst and
took him to the pediatrician. "We just about lived in
that doctor's office," said Carl. They asked the doctor
what to do. First he told them Keith was spoiled. "When
he cries, just leave him," the doctor said. "He'll cry
himself out. Just lock the door and leave him be." When
that didn't work, the doctor changed his prescription.
"Spank him," the doctor said.

Time after time, Carl and Jane would return to the
pediatrician's office, and to spare the other parents and

children, they'd wait in the hall with Keith. There he'd scream, and then, sooner or later, office doors would open and heads would poke out. "What's wrong? What's wrong?" people would ask. Jane or Carl would stand there with Keith screaming between their legs. Keith looked like an ordinary little boy. Ordinary kids didn't scream like Keith unless they were in pain, and if they were, ordinary parents did something. But Carl and Jane had already tried everything. When the doors swung open and worried people asked what was wrong, all they could say was "Nothing." Keith kept screaming while they stood there. The expression on people's faces changed from alarm to disbelief to distrust. Eventually, the pediatrician would call them in and, for the hundredth time, they'd ask him what to do. Finally, one day, the doctor admitted he didn't know. "Take him to an allergist," he said, and wrote them a referral.

The allergist tested Keith. For two hours, they endured a series of skin pricks and screams. For $300 they learned that Keith had no allergies. It was their first, but not their last, useless encounter with an expert. From the allergist they went to a pediatric neurologist, and from the neurologist they went on to a psychologist. "Retarded," the specialists said, but to what degree and why, no one knew. Eventually, they ended up at Emory University for another psychological evaluation. They handed Keith over to the staff and waited. After an hour, a secretary called them in. They made the mistake of going through the wrong door. "They had Keith in a cage," Carl said. "They didn't want us to see it, but we did." "Wait a second, Carl," I said. "A cage with bars?" "Oh yeah," he said. "They had him in a crib with a cage over the top. Like an animal. That's how they treated him. He was real upset." "Profoundly mentally retarded" was Emory's evaluation. Keith was five years old. "Institutionalize him," the psychologists said. "There's nothing you can do for him." That's when the Smiths took Keith to an evangelist.

187

The evangelist was holding a prayer meeting in a huge public auditorium in downtown Atlanta. Every seat in the place was taken. Far in the back, Carl, Jane, and Keith sat and waited for a miracle. Keith began to make noises. Ushers warned them that they'd have to leave if the boy didn't keep quiet. Jane took Keith on her lap and he settled down. The evangelist announced he would heal the sick. First he called for the lame and the halt; then he called for the blind. People on stretchers, people on crutches, people with walkers, people who couldn't see crowded around him. He touched them. He called God's grace down on them. Then he called out for those possessed by devils. He would cast out the devils. Carl stood up and took Keith by the hand and led him down the aisle, but when they came near the stage the ushers turned them away. The service went on. Again the evangelist announced he would heal the sick. He called out for the lame, the halt, and the blind, and again they thronged the stage, and again he healed them. Again he announced he would cast out devils, and again Carl stood up and led Keith down the aisle, but again the ushers turned them away. The service continued. Once more the evangelist announced a healing. First the crippled, then the blind. Once more he called out for those afflicted in spirit. For a third time, Carl stood up and walked down the aisle with Keith. And for the third time, the ushers wouldn't let them near the evangelist. Carl led Keith back to their seats. Ushers began to hand out wicker baskets, asking for prayer offerings. That's when Carl said he turned to Jane and told her, "If we don't get out of here, I might have to punch someone." "I was an old country boy," Carl said to me. "I knew bullshit when I smelled it."

On holidays, they'd visit their relatives. Jane's mother and father made allowances for Keith, but none of her aunts and uncles did. If the gathering was at one of their houses, frozen smiles greeted the Smiths. Keith had begun to take off his clothes in public. He had never

188

learned to be toilet-trained. He still screamed. Jane's aunts tried to pretend he wasn't there. After the first long scream or the first "accident," though, the hostess would walk over to Jane. In her sweetest voice, she'd say, "Oh, dear—Keith must be getting tired. I know how crowds must upset him. It's just a shame you have to leave so soon, and just after you got here." In fast-food restaurants and shopping malls, strangers shunned them and employees asked them to leave. When Keith was eight, they tried to go on vacation with him. They went to Daytona Beach, but all Keith did was stand on the shore and scream. They left after a day.

As Keith grew older, he slept less. Carl installed a lock on the outside of his bedroom door. At night, they shut him in, but still he made noise. At work, Carl tried to explain why he was so tired all the time, but his foreman wasn't interested and his fellow workers couldn't or wouldn't understand. One Saturday, Carl and Keith were at a shopping mall. One of Carl's fellow workers caught sight of him and came over. Keith stood by quietly. "Is this your son?" the man asked. "He looks O.K. to me. The way you talked, you made him sound like he had two heads." The man tried to shake hands with Keith, but the boy looked through him. On Monday, back at work, the man began to make remarks about Carl. "He's just making up stories," the man said. "I met his kid. There's nothing wrong with him." Carl tried to explain that Keith looked normal, but that inside, he wasn't. "What is he? From outer space?" the man said. That's when Carl hit him in the face. "I hit him good," Carl said. "I would have hit him some more, but people broke up the fight." Years of frustration and anger drove Carl's fist into the man's face. Nothing had helped, not medicine, not religion, not family, not friends. "We started snapping," Carl said.

By the time Keith was nine, Carl and Jane had begun to fall apart. Living with Keith day and night had left them physically and emotionally ill. Carl didn't explain exactly what happened, but somehow Jane found a private psychiatric hospital that would accept Keith for treatment. "You mean you committed him?" I asked. Carl looked very sad. He nodded. "We had to," he said. Since there was no comparable public facility where they lived, Jane convinced her county to pay half the cost of Keith's care. Carl's medical insurance paid the rest. Keith alternated between sixty days spent in the hospital and forty-five days spent as an outpatient, a cycle that lasted a year. The hospital "taught" him not to take off his clothes by taping his shirt sleeves to his wrists, his pants legs to his ankles, and his belt around his waist. Once a week, Carl and Jane were allowed to visit him. Each time Keith saw them, he said a single word, which he repeated from the moment they met him to the moment they said goodbye. "Home?" Keith said as they sat with him, and "Home?" he said as he watched them leave, standing at the window of the door of his locked ward. "Home?" he said, over and over as he wept and they wept, weekend after weekend. Carl looked sadder and sadder as he told me this. "It was real hard for all of us," he said.

Carl didn't speak for a while and neither did I. I thought about the alternatives. I thought about what the National Socialists had done as soon as they gained control of Germany's public mental health facilities: euthanasia of hopelessly deranged and damaged wards of the state, first children, then adults, killed by lethal injection. "Life unworthy of life" is how the Nazis would have classified Keith. Carl and Jane would have been informed their son had died "during treatment." That sort of intervention was murder, but what about benign neglect? What about doing what parents had done long before Victor, the boy said to have been raised by wolves, was found in the forest in southern France? If the state or the county or Carl's medical insurance could have or would have paid for it, why didn't the Smiths just leave Keith in the locked ward? I asked Carl about that.

What he answered was a single word: "Love" was what he said. "Why didn't you leave Keith in the hospital?" I asked. "You and Jane were breaking down. The doctors had advised you to commit him. You'd actually done that. Why didn't you just keep him there?" Carl looked at me straight in the eye. He wasn't surprised by the question and he wasn't angered by it. He understood. "Because," he said. "Because we *loved* him. It was *love*. It was *love*. We *loved* him." Four times he used that word. Eskimos are said to have a dozen words for snow and Indians of the Southwest are said to have just as many words for maize. English, though, has only one opaque four-letter word for love, and that's what Carl repeated like a man hammering a nail into wood. The psychologists at Emory had put Keith in a cage; the evangelist had turned him away; the pediatrician had said to spank him; Keith's own great-aunts and -uncles had shunned him. Who else was there for Keith but Carl and Jane? Leaving him in the locked ward had broken their hearts. Keeping him at home that whole year might have irreparably damaged them, but guilt and longing for their child must have been harder to bear than sleeplessness, anger, and exhaustion. "Keith was *our* son," Carl said. "If we didn't take care of him, who would? Who'd care for him the way we would? We're his parents. No one else. We're all he's got. We're *it*." As I listened to Carl, I thought of a word other than "love." I thought of "fidelity." It was an ancient word; in Latin, it was *fides* and *fidelis*, faith and faithfulness, trust and honor, a word that described a bond that risked death. Inside Carl's love was something for which men died. The Marines had rejected the wrong man.

At the end of a year, the Smiths brought Keith home. He didn't take his clothes off anymore, and he'd learned to go to the bathroom, more or less on his own, but he'd developed new bad habits: he pinched people painfully hard; he pulled at his hair, and he'd begun to bite his own arm. The pinching was aggressive; the hair pulling 191 and biting were what psychologists called "self-stimu-lation." Carl couldn't quite explain it, but, somehow or other, during the year Keith was hospitalized, the public mental health facilities of the county where the Smiths lived had so rapidly improved that there was now a place for people like Keith to go to school. That place was called a "psycho-ed. center," a facility staffed by teach-ers trained to educate children suffering from a variety of severe emotional and intellectual disabilities. Neither a hospital nor a warehouse, the center existed to teach and train its students to live and learn in the normal world. On the first day of school, the Smiths introduced Keith to his new teacher. Keith made noises and pulled at his hair. He tried to pinch Carl and began to take off his shirt. His new teacher watched everything he did without a frown or a smile. "Give me a chance to work with Keith" was all she said. Deanna was her name. She had a master's degree in special education and a particular interest in autism. She was the best thing that had yet happened to Keith and his parents. She was smart, tough, and persistent. Her teaching method was something called "behavior modification," a system of logical consequences that used consistent rewards and punishments to gradually replace bad behaviors with good ones. For example, Keith had grown very fond of food. Meals, especially dinner, made him laugh with delight. Mealtimes became rewards; their delay or de-privation became punishments. If, during the school day, Keith pinched another student, Deanna would say to him, "Keith, you're going to have to stay with me after school. When I stay after school, I work, so you'll have to work too. I stay until nine at night and I don't eat dinner, so I'm afraid you'll have to stay with me and not eat dinner too. Maybe tomorrow, if you don't pinch people, you can go home on time." It was a method that sounded obvious, even old-fashioned, but its consistent application required both rigor and flexibility. Like a martial art that used an opponent's own momentum against him, behavior modification used a student's own appetites, good and bad, to change his actions. Within a year, Deanna had stopped Keith from pinching, pulling his hair, and biting his arm. "She even learned him," said Carl, "to tie his own shoes."

The best years of Keith's life—and his family's—began. Like a clear signal emerging from static, Keith's own nature emerged from the tangle of bad behaviors that, until he'd met Deanna, had characterized him. In the afternoons, he'd sit in front of the TV and fill the room with deep, boisterous belly laughs as he watched programs like *Family Feud* and *Wheel of Fortune*. At night, he'd listen to sad, slow gospel music sung by Elvis or Anne Murray and his eyes would fill with tears. Carl would draw Keith to him in an embrace so close, their foreheads touched. "I used to put my head right up against his," Carl said. "I'd get as close as I could and I'd look in his eyes and I'd say, 'Keith—what's going on in there?' I was trying to look inside. I'd say, 'Keith? You hear me? Look at me, son. Who are you? Where are you?' Because I knew he was in there." After three years with Deanna, Keith was admitted to a program for people classified as "moderately mentally retarded." "*Moderately*," Carl said. "Those people at Emory thought Keith was hopeless, but Deanna, she showed 'em!" Three afternoons a week, Keith and other students like him were taken to the local Marriott Hotel and, in the Marriott's basement, they were taught to load and unload commercial washing machines. For another three years, Keith went to school and learned his trade. He did so well that the hotel said it might hire him when he turned eighteen. For Carl and Jane, it was as if Keith had been promised early admission to Harvard.

At home, Keith's behavior began to change. He had always loved to run and jump and play. For five summers, Carl had worked an extra job as a driver's helper, delivering appliances for Sears, to earn enough money   193 to install a swimming pool in the backyard. Keith stopped swimming; he stopped running; he stopped walking. He'd come home from school, stretch out on the couch, and refuse to move. At school, his teachers began to find him sitting alone, weeping silently. "It was a real sad kind of weeping," Carl said. "We couldn't figure it out." They'd noticed, though, that Keith had bumped his leg and that the bump hadn't healed. They took him to the doctor. The doctor looked at the leg and said it was just a bump. But the bump didn't disappear. They took him back to the doctor, and this time he X-rayed Keith's leg. He found a tumor. He referred them to an orthopedist. The orthopedist made more X-rays. "Don't worry," he said. "It's probably benign, but we'll have to remove it and do a tissue study." Keith had never been to a hospital before. He was terrified of needles. To start an IV on him was a nightmare of screaming and kicking. The surgeon operated. Keith was put in a hip cast. They waited for the pathologist's report. For three days, Keith kept pulling at his cast. "Take it off, take it off, take it off," he kept repeating. The pathologist's report came back positive. Keith had bone cancer. "It's not that bad," said the doctor. "There's an eighty percent chance of cure. He'll have to stay in the cast for five months, though. We'll monitor him."

Every bit of progress Keith had made with Deanna was destroyed by the operation. He began to bite his arm again. He began to take off his clothes and pull out his hair. He was tormented by itching. He kept poking things down his cast. When it was finally removed, they found his leg had been rubbed raw in three places. They began physiotherapy. Five months later, he could run again. A month went by and he began to limp; a month more and he began to hobble. He was seventeen years old. He went back to the hospital. The cancer had spread to his knee and his ankle. This time, the operation lasted seven hours. It was the first of five. A steel rod was run from Keith's pelvis, down his thigh, into his leg. Another year passed. In April 1987, they discovered cancer in his pelvis. This time, they gave him six weeks of heavy radiation. The cancer disappeared, but every month Keith had to return to the hospital for a checkup.

Across the street from the hospital was a Wendy's hamburger restaurant. As a reward, after each checkup the Smiths took Keith there for lunch. The rod down Keith's leg made it difficult for him to sit. All the operations, the anesthesia, the drugs, the pain, and the confusion had caused Keith to so regress that he couldn't go to the bathroom by himself, let alone sit down and stand up from a toilet without help. When Keith needed to, Carl went with him. One day, when Carl did, a customer reported to the restaurant manager that he'd seen two men go into the same stall in the bathroom. The manager went to the men's room and walked up to Carl. "You enjoy watching another man go to the bathroom?" he asked him. Carl said to me, "I came real close to hitting him. I said, 'He's my *son!* It's none of your goddamn business anyway. Why don't you mind your own goddamn business! This boy needs my help!' " All the anger that Carl had lived with, from the time the evangelist had turned them away to the time he'd exploded at work, had returned. It returned again as he told me this story. "Keith's my son," he said. "He's twenty years old and he can't even wipe his own ass. Who's gonna do that for him? Who else is gonna do that for him but me? No one but me. Who's gonna take care of him? When he needs to be washed, who's gonna wash him? Who's gonna shave him? Who's gonna make sure he's dressed and his face is clean? Who? No one but me. I'm his father. If I don't, who will? You tell me." I said I didn't know.

Carl grew quiet. After a while, I asked him how Keith was—if the cancer had returned. "No," he said. "But I'd rest a lot easier if I knew there'd be someone there to take care of Keith after I was gone. That's what worries me: who'll take care of him when I'm not here anymore?" Carl grew quiet again and I thought about him and his son. Their birthdays were nearly the same. Keith was much worse off than Carl had ever been, but Carl understood him because of all he'd suffered, dropping out of school and wandering for so long. As to "wiping his ass": Carl cleaned toilets at GM, and he didn't mind telling stories about his uncle Ronald and the sawmill belt. "Carl?" I said. "Is that the purpose of your life?" "What?" he asked. "To take care of your son?" I answered. "Is that why you were set here? Is that what you want carved on your tombstone? 'He took care of his son.' Is that your purpose on earth?" Carl looked at me. He looked baffled. "I don't know," he said. "I thought about that, but I don't know."

All this time, as we'd talked, we'd sat on the screened porch behind Carl's house. The house had been empty: Jane was at work; Keith was at his school; his sister was at hers. Carl looked at his watch and stood up. "It's time for Keith to be getting back," he said. "Come on out and you can meet him." We walked through the house, out the side door, down the driveway to the street. A few minutes later, a yellow van pulled up to the curb and Keith climbed out. I caught my breath: he was a younger version of Carl. "Do you want to shake hands, Keith?" Carl asked. Keith raised his hand and I took it. "Hi," he said. I looked at his eyes. They were blue and they were alive. "Come on, Keith," said Carl. "Let's go inside." I walked with them back to the house. We stood outside and I thanked Carl. "See you again," I said. I walked down the drive to my car. As I climbed in, I turned to look at the two of them. Carl had put his arm around Keith's neck, over his shoulders. He waved goodbye and so did Keith, father and son, the living picture of an elemental bond. "A prime number," I thought as I started the engine. "Nothing but themselves and one."

* * *

The next Sunday, I spoke with Jane. Carl had taken Keith with him on errands; Keith's sister was visiting friends. The house was quiet. We sat in the living room, Jane on the sofa, I in the matching easy chair. The story Jane told was different from Carl's. Its peaks and valleys were the same, but the terrain in between wasn't. Jane's facts, dates, and details, the cause, effect, and significance of events, even the events themselves, were different in her narrative than in Carl's. From the moment Keith was born, Carl had been able to leave for work, but for nine years, from the time Jane brought Keith home from the hospital until the day the Smiths committed him to the locked ward, Jane had lived with her child morning and night. For the first four years of Keith's life, she had been able to go nowhere with him but doctors' offices. For the next five years, she'd had half-day, then full-day respites, but she had never been able to leave Keith unattended. He had marked her life with a pattern of lines that were finer, deeper, and more intricate than the grooves he'd cut into Carl. Mothers always know more about their offspring than fathers, but when a child is as damaged as Keith and when his disability is as chronic and enigmatic as autism, Jane's search for knowledge became a torment. Year after year, the diagnoses of Keith's condition changed, depending on the preconceptions of the specialists who examined him. Year after year, Jane persisted in her search, love informing her understanding, and understanding sustaining her love. In the end, like the recovery of someone thought to have been lost at sea, her final knowledge gave her comfort.

Jane's story of her childhood was very different from Carl's. She had grown up, snug, loved, and happy, the youngest child in a family of three brothers and a sister who were so much older than she that, as she grew, she had no rivals, only protectors. The countryside for miles around was settled with kinfolk, aunts, uncles, and in-laws with surnames like McClure and Rogers, small

independent farmers of Irish Protestant stock who pros-
pered in the good times and survived the bad by hard
work and thrift. Jane's grandfather, her father's father,
had risen above the average to become a rich landowner
and county sheriff, but his good fortune ended with the
Depression. Jane's father began as a bricklayer. In 1945,
a few months after Jane was born, he bought eighty
acres of land from his father, built a good, solid house
for his family with his own hands, and settled them
there. For several more years, Jane's father traveled, as
he had before she was born, following construction work
from site to site throughout the state. Then, when Jane
was six, her father came home to stay and the family
flourished as never before. Their own cows, hogs, and
cattle provided them with meat and milk; vegetables
came from their own garden. Jane's father built houses,
office buildings, and banks, near and far, but it was
Jane's mother who ran the business that kept cash
in the family's pockets: there had been a farmhouse on
the land before Jane's father had built one; that house
the family turned into an egg hatchery. By the time Jane
was ten, the family had added two more. All these,
Jane's mother managed. By the time Jane was sixteen,
the family owned several hundred hens; the eggs they
produced, case after case of them, Jane's brothers delivered to supermarkets in the county. The '57 Chevy
that Jane was driving when she met Carl had belonged
to each of her brothers in turn; the car came with an
egg route. As each brother graduated from high school,
car and egg route passed to the next youngest. Jane
inherited both and kept them until she married Carl.

In Jane's family, everyone finished high school, and
everyone worked. Her older sister married a rich farmer;
her youngest brother went to college, then found a job
with the federal government; her oldest brother moved
to Atlanta and went to work for GM; her middle brother
became a bricklayer, then returned to the farm and
added a hundred-acre cattle ranch to it. The story Carl

told of his boyhood was full of blank spots, wanderings, off-color jokes, and failure. When I asked Jane what she remembered most about her girlhood, she spoke of Sunday dinners in a house crowded with cousins, the air thick with the smell of fried chicken and biscuits and the sound of people laughing. After Keith was born, she lived off those memories and all the happiness of her girlhood like a squirrel in winter.

She married Carl after a high school romance that had lasted for years fell apart. At first, when she met him, she wasn't interested in Carl, but then, she said, she began to appreciate him for what he was. "What's that?" I asked. "Oh," she said, surprised, "he's very natural, down-to-earth; there's nothing false about him; he felt like family." She was nearly twenty-one when they married. They moved to Atlanta and she went to business school to learn IBM keypunching, the sixties equivalent of data processing. She found work keypunching orders and inventory at places like J. C. Penney. After three years of marriage, Carl said he wanted to start a family. Jane didn't want children. "Not so soon," she said. "I liked my freedom." Carl convinced her by promising her a home of her own. They bought a house in the suburbs and Jane got pregnant.

Her labor was hard. Keith weighed nearly eight pounds and came out covered with hair, hair in his ears, hair down his back; Jane had never seen anything like it. He left her torn up and sore, so sore she couldn't sit up in bed. Nearly as soon as he was born he threw his first tantrum, propelling himself from one side of his bassinet to the other. Jane had never seen a baby do that before. When the nurses brought him in to be fed, he had to be coaxed to take the bottle, and once he took it, he didn't seem to know what to do with it. When Jane brought him home, she began to notice other things he couldn't or wouldn't do: he didn't make eye contact with her, he didn't turn his head to her, and he never smiled in recognition of her. What he loved was 199 to be held. When she put him down, he cried. She held him for hours. She spent all her time with him. He slept very little; he spit out his food. He was fussy, temperamental, angry—content only when Jane held him. When he was nine months, he sat up. In this, he was normal.

A year after Keith was born, Jane discovered she was pregnant again. "I was very angry," she said. "I had my hands full with Keith and now I had another one on the way." At fourteen months, Keith walked. That, too, was normal, but walking enabled him to "get into things." Jane's pregnancy drained her; taking care of Keith exhausted her. "He was very dependent, very needy, very—volatile," she said. He had two emotions: anger and exasperation. He began to throw tantrums, but his tantrums were unpredictable. Jane couldn't understand why he was always so angry. She tried one strategy after another to prevent or circumvent or eliminate whatever seemed to upset him, but no matter what she did, something always set him off. She was always cringing, always anxious. Out of desperation, she began to take notes. "That's pretty unusual," I said. "I didn't know what else to do," she answered. "I thought maybe if I could find a pattern, I could stop it." What her notes revealed was that Keith's tantrums had no pattern. "The only pattern," she said, "was that they happened every day." At sixteen months, he began to wake up at four o'clock every morning. "I never got any rest," she said.

Jane's trips to the pediatrician began. She divided her time between holding Keith on her lap at home and holding him on her lap at the doctor's office. One day, though, she discovered something while sitting in the doctor's waiting room. "I began to draw pictures for him," she said. She did it to keep him quiet, but it worked better than anything she'd tried before. She'd draw a tree, ask him what it was, then tell him. She'd draw a house and do the same thing. Soon he began to repeat her words and, as he repeated them, he grew content. He loved to imitate her.

When Keith was two, his sister was born. By then, Keith had almost no spontaneous language. He could echo words, but on his own, he said only "baby," "bottle," "bite," "eat," Momma," and "Daddy." "He had fifteen words altogether," Jane said. His tantrums continued. Jane had bought him a simple five-piece jigsaw puzzle. He'd dump it out, then fit it together. The same piece always provoked him. Sometimes the piece fit in place, sometimes it didn't, but no matter, it was the piece itself that upset him. When he screamed the baby cried. The house was never quiet. "And," said Jane, "if you didn't watch him, he'd get himself in trouble." One afternoon she sat down and dozed off without knowing it. When she woke up, smoke was pouring out of the kitchen: Keith had put his plastic blocks in the oven and turned it on. The house was full of toxic fumes.

When Jane's daughter was four months old, she took Keith to the pediatrician one more time. "Something's *wrong*," she said, and this time the doctor agreed. The allergy test that Carl described came only after a visit to an audiologist and an ophthalmologist. Keith was three when he first saw a neurologist. The way some mothers keep report cards and graduation certificates, Jane keeps copies of all Keith's important medical and psychological evaluations. As she told me about Keith's encounter with the neurologist, she handed me a Xerox of the man's report. "Minimal brain damage characterized by developmental delay and hyperactivity" was the doctor's conclusion. For the hyperactivity, he prescribed a modest amount of Dexedrine, the first in a series of medications that would, as Keith grew into adulthood, come to include such powerful antipsychotics as Stelazine and Haldol. For Keith's speech and language problems, the man referred the Smiths to a well-known local private school whose tuition was so far beyond their means that he might as well have suggested they walk to the moon. As I finished reading that first report, Jane handed me a second. It was written by a psychologist. "Although Keith manifested a marked psycholinguistic impairment, it was possible," wrote the psychologist, "to rule out varieties of childhood psychoses, including autism [and] childhood schizophrenia [characterized by auditory and visual hallucinations]. . . . Mental retardation is, at this time, the diagnostic label of highest validity." In spite of what would prove to be the first of many incomplete or erroneous diagnoses, Keith's first psychologist did teach Jane a way to control Keith's behavior. "There is little doubt," the man concluded, "as to the mode of treatment—behavior modification." Or, as Jane said, "he showed me how to use M&Ms." "M&Ms?" I asked, thinking it was some sort of psychological abbreviation. Jane smiled. "You know," she said. " 'They Melt in Your Mouth, Not in Your Hands.' " We laughed. She explained, "Every time Keith did something good, I told him to open his mouth and popped in a candy."

Using that simple method of reward, Jane began to teach Keith to name the world. What had begun with drawings in the doctor's office, Jane expanded: she cut pictures out of magazines, set Keith on her lap and showed him a picture of an apple. "What is this, Keith?" she asked. "It's an apple," she answered. "Say 'apple,' " she said. "Ah-pull," repeated Keith, and onto his tongue she put an M&M. Next, she showed him the picture of a cow and when he repeated its name—"Cah-wow"—she gave him another piece of candy. In this way, she taught him hundreds of names. But she wasn't content: while leafing through a Sears catalogue, she saw a description of flash cards. "Teach Your Child to Read," announced the catalogue. The accompanying picture showed big cards printed with brightly colored letters. "Teach Letters, Then Words," read the catalogue copy. Seventeen years later, Jane could still repeat

to me the instructions included in the box of flash cards she bought: "Flash the card for thirty seconds, then pronounce the word. Put the card away. Wait one minute. Flash the card again and pronounce the word. Again, put the card away. Later, place the card where the child will be sure to see it. In the middle of the day, point to the card and ask, 'What does this say?' "

With the help of Sears and M&Ms, Jane was able to teach Keith one word a day. "First he learned his ABCs," said Jane, "then words. He was very quick, very fast, very alert. He could repeat things. 'Say the word, Keith,' I'd say, and he would." First he mastered ten words, then twenty, then thirty, then hundreds and hundreds of them, words for things, people, animals, parts of the body. By the time Keith was four, he could read at almost second-grade level. He never surpassed that for the rest of his life. No teacher—except Deanna, years later—taught Keith as much as Jane did between his third and fourth years. Jane had no special training; she had no special equipment or facilities. Love, pride, and desperation gave her all the expertise she needed. Today, some might label Keith's performance "echolalic," nothing but his echo of Jane's words; others might dismiss what she did as equivalent to animal training: teaching a circus pony to count with his hooves. But, all alone in her living room, Jane did teach Keith to name the world and read its words. She did what no teacher could or would do again for another ten years.

The M&Ms had no effect on Keith's other behaviors: Jane had to lock her cabinets to prevent him from tearing the labels off all her cans. When new neighbors moved in next door, she had to introduce herself by explaining Keith's screams: "We're not abusing him," she'd say. "Don't think that. It's just he has learning problems and he gets frustrated sometimes. But we don't want you to think we're hurting him or anything." That sort of introduction prevented people from calling 203 the police, but it also made Jane few new friends. Her daughter had begun to walk by the time she was six months old. The little girl was very dainty and very attentive. At fourteen months, she began to talk. Keith pulled her hair and pushed her for no apparent reason. His tantrums continued. Television became his only pacifier. *The Price Is Right* entranced him. Jane worried about Keith's temper and what it might do to her daughter. She felt lonely and guilty: lonely because Keith's behavior drove people away while it required her to be more vigilant; guilty because she thought she might have been responsible for his misfortune: "I smoked cigarettes when I was pregnant," she said. "Maybe that did it. Or maybe it was my genes. Maybe he'd inherited something from me." Her solution was to enroll Keith in a place called the Hi Hopes Readiness Center. It was a half-day preschool program funded by Jane's county's Department of Education for children with what psychologists called "behavior disorders."

Hi Hopes gave Jane her first freedom in four years, but for Keith it was a disaster. The staff classified him as severely mentally retarded and put him in a class of children who were uncontrollable. The effect was equivalent to putting a first-time offender in jail with professional criminals. Places like Hi Hopes were intended to teach social skills, but what Keith learned was how to pinch, pull his hair, and bite his arm. For three years, he remained there. Jane had no choice: Hi Hopes was the only publicly funded school for someone like Keith. All Jane could do was continue to protest the Center's classification of Keith as severely mentally retarded. When Keith entered his last year there, Jane's protests were officially acknowledged: a psychiatrist under contract with Jane's county was directed to reevaluate Keith and make a recommendation for his future treatment. With a derisive smile, Jane handed me the woman's report. It referred to Keith as "a child with unsocialized aggressive reaction of childhood . . . [suffering from] schizophrenia." "Keith walked around, clapped his hands, and talked to himself," said Jane. "He always did that. But that doctor thought he was hallucinating. She didn't know anything about him."

As a ward of the county, the boy who could sit happily on his mother's lap and identify hundreds of pictures and read hundreds of words was now considered crazy and transferred to a campus called the North Metro Children's Center. There, he was enrolled in a day school full of head bangers and self-mutilators. There, the staff gave him Stelazine. Soon he learned chest pounding, a new kind of bizarre behavior. His day school was in a building that had no bathrooms of its own, so Keith's toilet training quickly degenerated. On the days when Jane came to pick him up at school, she passed through the main building of the campus, a residential center for children who had "graduated" from Keith's day school. "The place was a zoo," Jane said. Its walls were smeared with food; screams and shouts filled the air; children walked around wearing football helmets to prevent them from injuring themselves when they pounded their heads against walls. Jane became frightened: Keith was nine years old. He had made no progress since he was four. His tantrums had grown worse. His chest pounding, hair pulling, and arm biting continued. Unless Jane could think of something to do to help him, he might "graduate" like the others.

Help came from a comment made by one of Keith's teachers. Keith's behavior, said the teacher, reminded her of another child she'd seen, a child who had been diagnosed as autistic. The teacher gave Jane the telephone number of the child's mother. The two women talked for hours. "At last," Jane said, "I knew what was wrong with Keith." He wasn't a fool and he wasn't a lunatic: he suffered from an enigma. Jane joined the local Society of Children and Adults with Autism. "It was my first step out of the maze." The Society had a small library, supplemented with a suggested reading 205 list. Jane read and talked to more parents of autistic children. What she read and heard enabled her to see the pattern she'd been looking for since she first took notes on Keith's earliest tantrums. The chaos of his behaviors cohered. Her relief came not just from knowing what he was, but from knowing what he wasn't. The "zoo" wasn't his destiny.

Parents of other autistic children told Jane about the private psychiatric hospital where the Smiths committed Keith. Hospitalizing him was a desperate act: Hi Hopes had neglected him; his day school had done little more than babysit him; the residential center that would have been his future might have destroyed him. The Smiths visited Keith's hospital three times each week: one day for family counseling, one day for a parents' support group, and one day, Sundays, to see their son. Sundays broke Jane's heart. Mother and son had never been separated for so long before. The hospital's locked ward weaned them from each other. For the first time since Keith was born, Jane was free of him; she felt relief, but also loneliness and guilt. To escape her sadness, Jane looked for a job. What she found was four hours a day working the cash register at Burger King. Her keypunch experience served her well. The pay was good; the work satisfied her. Even after Keith was released, she kept the job. She has it still. She's been at it ten years, now working full-time, one rank below assistant manager. The most experienced employee in her restaurant, she's in charge of all "front of the house" operations.

The local Autism Society had told Jane that federal law required her county to pay for half of Keith's hospital care. She and the county's bureaucrats worked out an arrangement: each time Keith changed from being an inpatient to an outpatient, Jane was to notify them by phone. In August 1979, she called her county's Department of Education to tell them that Keith was about to begin his next hospital stay and that they should be ready to pay the next set of bills. They answered that, according to law, they had fulfilled their obligations and were no longer responsible for Keith's medical care. Jane said Keith was screaming in the living room while they told her this. She said she took the phone from her ear and held it up, over her head, pointed in Keith's direction so that the bureaucrat on the other end could hear the screams. "Can you hear that?" she said to him. "Can you hear that goddamn screaming? I'm going to take you to court if you don't do something for Keith. I'm going to take him to school. School's going to start in a month. I'm going to put him in the car and take him to school and *leave* him in your goddamn parking lot. I'm going to let your teachers have him for a day and we'll see how they deal with it." That tirade was enough, said Jane, to convince the bureaucrat that the woman he was listening to was just angry enough to do what she threatened.

Federal law did require Jane's county to do more than the bureaucrat said it would, but there were gaps—not just between what the law required and what funds were actually available to meet those requirements, but between the law and the number of facilities actually built to accommodate children with multiple handicaps, and between the law and the number of teachers and paraprofessionals actually trained to teach, tutor, and care for physically and mentally disabled children. From Hi Hopes to the North Metro Children's Center to the telephone conversation with the bureaucrat, Jane and Keith had been climbing a ladder of special schools and mental health facilities, rung by rung, at the very moment those rungs were being added by the county where they lived. Which is why, after Jane's tirade, the man on the other end of the line replied, "Hang on. Calm down. We can't pay Keith's hospital bills anymore but what we can do is enroll him at a psycho-ed. center. It just opened." It was a matter of timing: at the moment Jane reached for the next rung for her son to cling to, that 207 rung—in the form of a special facility and a highly trained teacher named Deanna—was there.

What followed, said Jane, were "the three best years of our lives." By Keith's third year with Deanna, the boy who had spoken only in single-word sentences—if he spoke at all—was standing at a microphone, in a school pageant, singing Christmas carols. Instead of giving Keith Stelazine, Deanna took him out into the world and gave him practice ordering food in a restaurant or buying candy in a convenience store. The Smiths began to live lives that were nearly normal. "You have no idea!" said Jane, laughing at the memories. "We could actually go out at night—the whole family—and *stand in line* at a Red Lobster! We could stand and wait our turn *like everyone else!* We'd never been able to do that before. Or we could go to church and *sit through the whole sermon* without Keith throwing a fit. Or we could sit in the bleachers at our daughter's Little League game and Keith would *just sit there* and *cheer along with us!*" The simplest pleasures exhilarated them. Like amputees fitted with new limbs, the Smiths marveled at their ability to move through the world. At age thirteen, Keith graduated from the psycho-ed. center and was admitted to a special classroom in an ordinary public school. "It was pure triumph!" said Jane, laughing again. Two more wonderful years followed: Keith learned how to sit at a desk; how to use a scissors to cut a straight line, how to sort things according to size and shape. Then the Marriott accepted him in its training program. He learned how to follow instructions and work on his own. He stopped screaming; he slept better at night.

Six years of the most ordinary kinds of happiness ended when he got cancer. Jane told me all the hospital stories Carl had: the fear and the screams; the first operation and the hip cast; the first relapse and all the long, gruesome operations that followed. Through it all, Jane stayed with Keith, slept near him, held his hand, rubbed his neck, patted his back, rubbed his head, touched him and held him so that even at the worst moments, he could feel she was there.

It had taken most of the day for Jane to tell me her story, and nearly an hour for her to recount Keith's cancer. By then, it was late afternoon and the light in the room had grown dim. Neither of us had moved from our places since morning, Jane on the sofa, I in the easy chair. She was, in full face and profile, a most ordinary-looking woman, slim, short-haired, neither plain nor unattractive, pleasing to look at but unremarkable. This is how she appeared to me when I first saw her. But as the day went on and her story continued and I grew more amazed by what she had done and endured for the sake of her son, her appearance changed. As I looked and listened to her, hour after hour, she became beautiful to me. I was glad, when the light faded, that she couldn't see my face. I was glad because my expression would have unsettled her and embarrassed me, would have betrayed my feelings. The only word I have to describe them is the blunt four-letter word that Carl had used, over and over, to explain why he had abided with Keith. Love was what I felt for Jane, but it had less to do with desire than with admiration. Whether Jane's telling me her story actually changed her appearance or whether the effect of her story so changed me that I came to see her differently, I truly don't know. What I do know is that, as she reached the end of her story, I was listening as carefully as I had ever listened to anyone.

When, in the spring of 1987, the cancer had spread to Keith's pelvis and the doctors had fought it with heavy radiation, they'd ordered follow-up scans by a nuclear magnetic resonance device. Jane described the machine as if it were a gigantic cannon, lying on its side; for it to work, a patient had to be inserted into it, slid, horizontally, like an artillery shell down its bore. Keith refused to lie down on the machine's gurney. The prospect of being slid down the muzzle of the machine terrified him. "It won't hurt; it won't hurt," the attendants told him, but he pushed them away. Jane had been with him until then. "We can't get him to lie down," the attendants said. "I'll lie down next to him," she answered. She changed into a hospital gown. Mother and son lay down side by side. With her next to him, they slid down the tunnel of the enormous machine and, together, they were scanned.

That was the last story Jane told me, except to say that Keith was better now. In five years, she said, Carl would be eligible for his pension from GM. Then they'd sell their house and move back to North Carolina, back to her parents and her happy memories. Her home state had one of the best public health programs in the whole country for autistic people. It had group homes for adults like Keith. In five years, she said, they'd move back to North Carolina, settle Keith in a group home, and visit him every weekend. "That's what we hope anyway," she said. I'd thought of everything she'd gone through to reach that hope, all the pain and isolation, all the satisfactions and disappointments, all the anger, loneliness, and triumphs, and I didn't know what to say. As Carl and I had sat in silence when he'd finished telling me his story, and as—before that—Hollis Watkins and I had sat without speaking in the gravel parking lot of a church in Mississippi, now Jane and I sat without talking, she still on the sofa, I still in the easy chair. I kept thinking of her lying next to Keith, sliding down the barrel of that enormous machine, and as I thought, I wondered. "Jane?" I said. "Have you ever read the Book of Job? It just seems that . . ." She interrupted me. "Oh yes," she said. "I've read it. Many times."

Epilogue

THERE ARE a number of ways to explain all this. Neu-
rologists might say that empathy is a function of the
limbic system of the brain, that it's as "hard-wired" as
a fight-or-flight response, that it's as reflexive as a knee
jerk. Sociologists have theorized that altruism is a behavior inherited from early *Homo sapiens* who banded
together in small kinship groups: since the groups were
extended families, self-sacrifice ensured the survival of
the common gene pool. Survival of the fittest, say the
sociobiologists, was impossible without altruists. There
are even moral philosophers and educators who claim
to have proof that children's moral reasoning parallels
their cognitive development, that as children's brains
grow, so do their consciences.

All these explanations are abstract enough to apply
to everyone, but not specific enough to explain why
Curtis Sliwa ran into a burning building when he was
fifteen or why Hollis Watkins, safe and sound in LA,
decided to return to Mississippi. Carl Smith said to me
that if Keith died before him, he'd ask the doctors to
autopsy his brain to find out why Keith behaved as he
did. Perhaps when Carl dies, doctors could do the same 211

thing to him. Perhaps they'd discover his limbic system was more highly developed than normal. Until then, though, how would a sociobiologist or a moral philosopher explain Carl's fidelity?

There are more ways to dismiss the stories in this book than to explain them. As a representative sample of the population of the United States—let alone the world—the nine people in this book are too much of one thing and too little of another. There are far too many Catholics, lapsed or otherwise, among them; far too many are members of the working class, and far too many are men. To write this book, I interviewed thirty people and talked to twice as many more. I could pretend I was a fisherman and tell you about the ones that got away. I could impersonate a film editor and point to the tangles at my feet. Still, that wouldn't explain why I chose to write about the people I did. The best explanation is that their stories made sounds I could hear and colors I could see. In this, I was no better or worse than a dog, confined to a certain spectrum, alert to only a certain range of frequencies. The truth in this book isn't the whole truth, but even as a fragment, what does it mean?

What it means—if heroism is defined as rescue—is that heroism is a conjunction of opposites. Seen from a distance, heroism appears to be an act of self-sacrifice; experienced from within, it is also an act of self-reclamation. The hero rescues his own self as he rescues another. Heroes are able because they are disabled; generous because they know they're selfish; fearless because they know they're cowards. They succeed because of all the times they've failed; they win because of all their losses. Heroism is a dialectic: all the bad a hero knows about himself collides, in his conscience, with all the good he hopes to be. Edward V. Roberts is a clear example of such a hero: giving and getting, loss and mastery, fear and acceptance, ebb and flow in him like 212 blood pumping through a heart.

Epilogue

The sinister and shameful part of a man is easy enough to understand and articulate, but a man's good is irreducible. Like hope at the bottom of Pandora's box, it is often all that remains after he's lost everything else. Rosser couldn't even die when he wanted; Murphy had never felt so scared or so guilty; Chorcoran was an aimless but amiable loser; Mosher couldn't even jump-start his own cab. Sliwa had been either an outsider or a victim most of his life; Roberts had been treated like a dog that had been hit by a car; Watkins lived in a war zone with no weapons but his voice. All of them were desperate. And the Smiths? What special knowledge and what plentiful resources did they have to help their son? Flash cards from Sears? A job cleaning toilets at GM? How did they, how did any of the people in this book, manage to save anyone else? Carl Smith with an arm around Keith's neck; Jane Smith lying next to her son as they slid into the machine—their gestures embody the answer. It's that simple four-letter word Carl kept repeating. It's as clear and common as your face in the mirror.